בטח

the P R O M I S E

A 31-Day Devotional on Confidence
WALK BOLDLY WITH GOD

...and surely I am with you always, to the very end...

Matthew 20:28

stephanie d. moore

It is the Lord who goes before you.
He will be with you; he will not leave you or
forsake you. Do not fear or be dismayed.

Deuteronomy 31:8

בטח

the P R O M I S E

stephanie
d. moore

In Loving Memory

Charles "Willie" Oakley

This is what Hezekiah did throughout Judah, doing what was good and right and faithful before the Lord his God. In everything that he undertook in the service of God's temple and in obedience to the law and the commands, he sought his God and worked wholeheartedly. And so he prospered.

2 Chronicles 31:20-21

Introduction

While God makes many promises to us throughout the Bible, there is one enduring promise that is perhaps the most important.

When I was in my late thirties I wrote a book, entitled 'Echoes'. It is an autobiography of life before I turned 37. In 'Echoes', at the end of every chapter, was a recognition of "the heartbeat that remained", which I realized was God. In my darkest moments God has always been there, he is my heartbeat.

This is the promise. God will never leave us nor forsake us. He goes before us and he is with us. He is our Alpha and our Omega, the beginning and the end.

God is life. This recognition comes through confident reflection, the re-evaluation of our experiences, which eventually guide us to an authentic appreciation for a relationship with our Savior, Jesus Christ.

God is there when we celebrate our victories alone, when we finish arduous projects without acknowledgement or gratitude. God is there when we sin privately and drown in guilt. God is there when we feel helpless, unloved, unwanted, and unfit. God promises to always be wherever we are.

This should give us an abundance of peace, but often, despite our knowledge and awareness of it, it doesn't. This is why I titled the book, **בטח**. In the Hebrew, this means "the promise" but it also means, "to trust" or "have confidence in". This is what God desires - that we trust and place our confidence in Him.

How do we get there? Well, the truth is, as we grow in our relationship with God, we have trust in Him, but at times, our emotions take the wheel. We can't help but see the destruction that lies at our doorstep, the sense of fear that creeps in uncertainty, or the hate fueled by others making us feel small and unwanted.

Much like our heartbeat, we can only learn to rely on God moment-by-moment, day-by-day, and inch-by-inch. Our goal is to wake up each day and simply trust him today.

"It is the Lord who goes before you.
He will be with you; he will not leave you or forsake
you. Do not fear or be dismayed."

Deuteronomy 31:8

1

Love

For God so loved the world that he gave his one and only Son, that whoever believes in him shall not perish but have eternal life.

John 3:16

Love is an action, grounded in intentionality, comforted by consistency, and fortified by the heart that holds it. God is.

Action

It is not ironic that the symbol of love is often indicated by a heart. The physical heart's job when it functions properly is to continue (it never stops) that we may live, regardless of condition.

The heart is made up of four chambers, a heartbeat, and blood vessels. Each area has specific responsibilities to support a healthy body. The four chambers and our blood vessels ensure we have plenty of oxygen in our blood and our heart beats more than 100,000 times a day operating the valves of blood flow. (1)

"Indeed, he who watches over Israel will neither slumber nor sleep."

Psalm 121:4

Intentionality

Love creates intentional pathways by which to bless. Much like the diversification of the heart, God has ordained portions of himself to ensure each of us, individually and collectively, are in some way connected to his person.

Love is always given and received. A person must be intentional to give it, but the person who receives it may not be aware.

"Here I am! I stand at the door and knock. If anyone hears my voice and opens the door, I will come in and eat with that person, and they with me."

Revelations 3:20

Consistency

The best service we receive is the service we never have to question. We know the intention of the service is to be reliable, and just knowing the intention, helps us to put every situation we encounter into context.

While God serves us, he is not a service provider. He is our Heavenly Father and his love is consistent. God is faithful. He is always available. He is always aware. God loves us. Therefore, when situations arise that do not reflect the character of his actions or align with his intentions, we can look at the consistency of God and recognize that his love is at work in every circumstance.

"Humble yourselves, therefore, under God's mighty hand, that he may lift you up in due time. Cast all your anxiety on him because he cares for you. Be alert and of sober mind. Your enemy the devil prowls around like a roaring lion looking for someone to devour."

I Peter 5:6-8

Fortified

There is indeed something special about feeling secure. Security provides confidence. We are confident when we trust our most prized possession(s) to a bank or institution who has committed to care for it. Security

affords us the freedom to choose.

When we trust God, we entrust our soul, our beliefs,

and our will to Him.

*"Trust in the Lord with all your heart and lean not
on your own understanding; in all your ways submit
to him, and he will make your paths straight."*

Proverbs 3:5-6

God's promise is not only to be with us at all times,

but to love us at all times. He is intentionally consistent

and committed to ensuring that we are not only safe, but

that we are also going in the right direction.

Prayer

Most Gracious and Heavenly Father.

Thank you. Your presence shifts the atmosphere
and our recognition of your presence
provides security. Your love is greater than
any love we may receive from man.

So we have come to know and to believe the love
that God has for us. God is love, and whoever abides
in love abides in God, and God abides in him. (2)

You promised that when we seek you with all of our
heart, we will find you. (3) And that when we draw
near to you, you will draw near to us. (4) For surely the
righteous will give thanks to your name; the upright
will dwell in your presence. (5) You are with us and will
keep us wherever we go, and will bring us back to this
land. For you will not leave us until you have done what
you have promised us. (6) One thing I have asked of
the Lord, that I will seek after: that I may dwell in the
house of the Lord all the days of my life, to gaze upon
the beauty of the Lord and to inquire in his temple. (7)

In Jesus Name, Amen.

2

Strength

Fear not, for I am with you; be not dismayed, for I am your God; I will strengthen you, I will help you, I will uphold you with my righteous right hand.

Isaiah 41:10

Strength has many meanings. When God says he is with us, in the complexity of his personhood, we can appreciate every implied definition of the term, strength.

Physical/Material

I remember moving from my rental property into my new home. I was so happy but I was all alone. I did not have one person in my life that could help me. When it came to moving large furniture and when I would get to the end of my physical will (because I was so tired), I would pray to God to allow the Holy Spirit to help me.

I promise you, in those moments, just praying for his strength gave my body a will I could not fathom. But more practically speaking, God is always with us and he knows everything we endure. He also knows what we need. While he may not give us physical strength, he will give us the wisdom to call strength in the room. I later called movers to complete what I could not! I am thankful I was strong enough to submit to and financially afford the better plan.

> *"Seek the Lord and his strength; seek his presence continually!"*
>
> *I Chronicles 16:11*

Political/Social

When we are able to put the "meat on the bone" so to speak in a situation, we are entering that space with strength, and political power. Every room we walk into with God on our side, we have already activated an invisible power structure and it is at work. God is going before us and making every crooked place straight, he is carving out a path for us, he is placing the right people in the room and the right desires in our heart.

*"Be watchful, stand firm in the faith,
act like men, be strong."*

I Corinthians 16:13

Mentally Emotionally

Mental strength requires belief and trust in God. When we exercise our faith muscle, it develops into an undeniable trust in God and we believe God. We can see a situation through the lens of God as opposed to the lens of man. This sober reflection also tempers any frantic thoughts, illogical or logical arguments, and replaces them with a higher emotional IQ. The blessing of God's presence is that he takes our mustard seed of faith and moves mountains. The more we exercise this muscle our mental and emotional abilities diversify, capacities increase, and our capabilities are strengthened. This form of resilience is only afforded to us who bask in the presence of God and are unshakable in our beliefs.

*To the choirmaster. A Psalm of David, the servant of
the Lord, who addressed the words of this song to
the Lord on the day when the Lord delivered him*

from the hand of all his enemies, and from the hand of Saul. He said: I love you, O Lord, my strength. The Lord is my rock and my fortress and my deliverer, my God, my rock, in whom I take refuge, my shield, and the horn of my salvation, my stronghold.

Psalm 18:1-2

Abstract/Theoretical

The simple matter is that when we meet people who walk with God, we cannot help but believe, there is simply "something special" about them. Take David, a shepherd boy, working the fields, minding his own business, when one day he is anointed. Only God knew that David worshipped him, the others did not. David, in his intimate moments, honored God through his worship, his actions, and his praise. David walked with an "inner force" one that was greatly admired but not readily interpreted as one being enveloped by the presence of God.

Then he said to me, "This is the word of the Lord to Zerubbabel: Not by might, nor by power, but by my Spirit, says the Lord of hosts."

Zechariah 4:6

God's promise is not only to be with us at all times, but to give us strength at all times. He is going to strengthen us in every way: mentally, emotionally, physically, spiritually, and financially.

Prayer

Most Gracious and Heavenly Father.

Thank you. Your presence shifts the atmosphere and our recognition of your presence provides security. Your love is greater than any love we may receive from man.

The Lord is my strength and my shield; in him my heart trusts, and I am helped; my heart exults, and with my song I give thanks to him. The Lord is the strength of his people; he is the saving refuge of his anointed. (8)

But he said to me, "My grace is sufficient for you, for my power is made perfect in weakness." Therefore I will boast all the more gladly of my weaknesses, so that the power of Christ may rest upon me. For the sake of Christ, then, I am content with weaknesses, insults, hardships, persecutions, and calamities. For when I am weak, then I am strong. (9)

And you shall love the Lord your God with all your heart and with all your soul and with all your mind and with all your strength. (10)

In Jesus Name, Amen.

3

Jealousy

You shall not bow down to them or serve them, for I the Lord your God am a jealous God, visiting the iniquity of the fathers on the children to the third and the fourth generation of those who hate me.

Exodus 20:5

The jealousy God carries for us is like that of a protective father; he knows who we are and what we have the potential to become with his guidance, love, and provision. When someone or something threatens our well being, his jealousy becomes evident to all involved.

The Philistines

Samson was most notably the strongest man in the Bible. He was afforded his strength by God with the sole purpose of defeating the Philistines and punishing them for the way they treated the Jews, God's chosen people.

Samson fell in love with a Philistine woman. But his love for her was planted by God. In this way, he was able to find offense in the Philistines and punish them for many salacious acts.

His father and mother replied, "Isn't there an acceptable woman among your relatives or among all our people? Must you go to the uncircumcised Philistines to get a wife?"

But Samson said to his father, "Get her for me. She's the right one for me." (His parents did not know that this was from the Lord, who was seeking an occasion to confront the Philistines; for at that time they were ruling over Israel.)

Judges 14:3-4

Jezebel

Jezebel was a powerful woman married to the King of Samaria, Ahab. She refused to worship God and she led many in the kingdom to worship a false god called Baal. In doing so, she planned and plotted the murder of many prophets and spiritual leaders. God, through the prophet Elijah, prophesied a horrific death for her, and it came to pass exactly as predicted.

"And also concerning Jezebel the Lord says: 'Dogs will devour Jezebel by the wall of Jezreel.' (There was never anyone like Ahab, who sold himself to do evil in the eyes of the Lord, urged on by Jezebel his wife. He behaved in the vilest manner by going after idols, like the Amorites the Lord drove out before Israel.)

I Kings 21:23, 25-26

"Throw her down!" Jehu said. So they threw her down, and some of her blood spattered the wall and the horses as they trampled her underfoot. Jehu went in and ate and drank. "Take care of that cursed woman," he said, "and bury her, for she was a king's daughter." But when they went out to bury her, they found nothing except her skull, her feet and her hands. They went back and told Jehu, who said, "This is the word of the Lord that he spoke through his servant Elijah the Tishbite: On the plot of ground at Jezreel dogs will devour Jezebel's flesh.Jezebel's body will be like dung on the ground in the plot at Jezreel, so that no one will be able to say, 'This is Jezebel.'"

2 Kings 9:33-37

Judas

Judas Iscariot betrayed Jesus Christ which led to the culmination of God's divine plan for our salvation. Judas was a man led by greed. In his greed, he worked with the enemy of God to stop the growth of the church, and the worship of Jesus Christ. There are two accounts of Judas' death in the Bible. One describes his fatal act of suicide, the other describes what can believed to be result of his suicide (the act of his body falling from the noose with his decomposed body exposed for all to see). But without contradiction, the anguish of his guilt consumed him and what he thought would make him happy, in the end, did not.

When Judas, who had betrayed him, saw that Jesus was condemned, he was seized with remorse and returned the thirty pieces of silver to the chief priests and the elders. "I have sinned," he said, "for I have betrayed innocent blood."

"What is that to us?" they replied. "That's your responsibility."

So Judas threw the money into the temple and left. Then he went away and hanged himself.

The chief priests picked up the coins and said, "It is against the law to put this into the treasury, since it is blood money." So they decided to use the money to buy the potter's field as a burial place for foreigners. That is why it has been called the Field of Blood to this day. Then what was spoken by Jeremiah the prophet was fulfilled: "They took the thirty pieces of silver, the price set on him by the people of Israel, and they used them to buy the potter's field, as the Lord commanded me."

Matthew 27:3-10

The Philistines, Jezebel, and Judas

The common thread that is woven through the stories of the Philistines, Jezebel and Judas is that there was a clear enemy of God wreaking havoc among his people in an attempt to change their minds about God and his sovereignty. When anyone or any system sets itself up against the belief of God, it has no power and in fact terminates its usefulness to society. God is a jealous God and he will always get his revenge.

"Thus says the Lord of hosts: I am jealous for Zion with great jealousy, and I am jealous for her with great wrath."

Zechariah 8:2

God's promise is not only to be with us at all times, but to assure us He is fully aware of the enemy's actions and intentions. Vengeance belongs to God and He will repay.

Prayer

Most Gracious and Heavenly Father,

Thank you. Your presence shifts the atmosphere
and our recognition of your presence
provides security. Your love is greater than
any love we may receive from man.

The Lord is a jealous and avenging God; the Lord is
avenging and wrathful; the Lord takes vengeance
on his adversaries and keeps wrath for his enemies.
(11) Therefore, I will not fret because of evildoers;
nor be envious of wrongdoers! For they will soon
fade like the grass and wither like the green herb.
I will trust in the Lord, and do good; dwell in the
land and befriend faithfulness. (12) For the Lord our
God in our midst is a jealous God—lest the anger
of the Lord our God be kindled against us, and he
destroy us from off the face of the earth. (13)

So we set the Lord as a seal upon our heart, as
a seal upon our arm, for love is strong as death,
jealousy is fierce as the grave. Its flashes are
flashes of fire, the very flame of the Lord. Many
waters cannot quench love, neither can floods
drown it. If a man offered for love all the wealth of
his house, he would be utterly despised. (14)

In Jesus Name, Amen.

4

Confidence

*For the Lord will be your confidence and
will keep your foot from being caught.*

Proverbs 3:26

Confidence requires trust in someone, something,
or in one self.

Sufficiency is from God

God allows us to gain the right skills, the proper
perspective, the appropriate connections, and a humble
heart that we may do his will in the spaces he has
ordained for us to be in. At times, the doors he opens are
unbelievable and may cause us to suffer from imposter
syndrome or give us a moment of uncertainty. But the
presence of God gives us clarity to move forward in
confidence. God is a solid rock on which we can stand.

So we can confidently say, "The Lord is my helper;
I will not fear; what can man do to me?"

Hebrews 13:6

Laying Our Burdens Down

We will have days that are filled with burdensome activities. Moments when we must report in confidence despite the lack of information, confirmation, or determination. These are opportunities to encourage ourselves in the Lord. These are the challenges that require us to have greater faith and trust in God. In those moments, we can depend on God to grant us wisdom, discernment, and beloved protection to guide every action and every conversation.

Indeed, we felt that we had received the sentence
of death. But that was to make us rely not on
ourselves but on God who raises the dead.

2 Corinthians 1:9

Choose God

Jesus died so that we may have direct access to God through prayer and worship. When that unmitigated access was granted, we no longer had to perform specific rituals or be ordained to enter the Holy of Holies, we were welcome through our acceptance of Jesus Christ as our Savior. Therefore, our reliance on man is negated by our reliance on God. Man cannot do, see, or protect the way that God does. Man does not love us unconditionally as God does. Despite what man may promise, or seem to be, God will always have the final say. With this knowledge, it is important that we choose and desire God. After all, he loved us before we even realized who we were or what we might become. Any access we may have to persons with power or authority (and vice versa) was first allowed by God himself.

Blessed is the man who trusts in the Lord, whose trust is the Lord. He is like a tree planted by water, that sends out its roots by the stream, and does not fear when heat comes, for its leaves remain green, and is not anxious in the year of drought, for it does not cease to bear fruit.

Jeremiah 17: 7-8

God's promise is not only to be with us at all times,

but to shower us with his confidence that we may face

any situation in wisdom with peace.

Prayer

Most Gracious and Heavenly Father,

Thank you. Your presence shifts the atmosphere
and our recognition of your presence
provides security. Your love is greater than
any love we may receive from man.

And I am sure of this, that he who began a good
work in us will bring it to completion at the day
of Jesus Christ. (15) I have confidence in the Lord
that we will take no other view, and the one who is
troubling us will bear the penalty, whoever he is. (16)
Therefore, we must be all the more diligent to confirm
our calling and election, for if we practice these
qualities we will never fall. (17) Blessed is the man
who trusts in the Lord, whose trust is the Lord. (18)

In Jesus Name, Amen.

5

Peace

Peace I leave with you; my peace I give to you. Not as the world gives do I give to you. Let not your hearts be troubled, neither let them be afraid.

John 14:27

Peace is the gift that the Lord gives to those who choose Him as their Savior. It is only when we let go and truly trust God that we grasp hold of this gift.

God is in our Gratitude

Life is complex and our responsibilities are often laborious, leaden, and lethargic. If we aren't careful, we will find ourselves complaining about life rather than praising God for our appreciation of life. There is always a reason to praise Him, and our gratitude welcomes the presence of God. Our gratitude is a form of worship that indicates our love, dependence, and belief that God always has our best interest at heart.

> *But thou art holy, O thou that*
> *inhabitest the praises of Israel.*
>
> Psalm 22:3

Rest

If you have ever bought a home, you can understand how nerve racking it can be! From being qualified to waiting to see if your offer was the one accepted, to the inspection process - it is an emotional roller coaster. I had to buy a home in 60 days! That was one the craziest and most stressful experiences of my life, next to bearing children and getting married. The only thought that gave me peace was knowing God was with me. Regardless of our circumstance, God is with us in every moment. Sometimes, it requires us to take a spiritual inventory in real time to help us get through.

> *Do not be anxious about anything, but in every*
> *situation, by prayer and petition, with thanksgiving,*
> *present your requests to God. And the peace of*

*God, which transcends all understanding, will
guard your hearts and your minds in Christ Jesus.*

Philippians 4:6-7

Protection

When Jesus realized the time had come for Him
to sacrifice His life so that we may obtain it, the situation
made Him so nervous that He sweated blood. Jesus'
greatest desire was to have someone, anyone of His
disciples to pray with Him in those final moments. But
God required Him to face that circumstance with God
himself, and only God by his side.

When we are faced with accusatory, defaming, and
life threatening circumstances the emotions that come
like tides to shore are betrayal, heartbreak, loneliness,
shame, and perhaps anger. Yet, we are not alone. In fact,
we have a cadre of witnesses to see how in the face of
fear, we stand on faith and continue to trust God despite
our circumstances. In a state of fear, we can still obtain

God's rest because we know who holds tomorrow.

*For I am the Lord your God who takes hold of your
right hand and says to you, Do not fear; I will help you.*

Isaiah 41:13

God's promise is not only to be with us at all times,

but to arise in glory as we praise him for his rest and

protection that result in abundant peace.

Prayer

Most Gracious and Heavenly Father,

*Thank you. Your presence shifts the atmosphere
and our recognition of your presence
provides security. Your love is greater than
any love we may receive from man.*

*Now may the Lord of peace himself give us peace at
all times and in every way. The Lord be with all of us.
(19) For you will keep in perfect peace our minds which
stay on you, because we trust in you.(20) Surely God is
our salvation; we will trust and not be afraid. The LORD,
the LORD himself, is our strength and our defense;
he has become our salvation. (21) Let the peace of
Christ rule in our hearts, since as members of one body
we were called to peace. And we are thankful. (22)*

In Jesus Name, Amen.

6

Protection

You are a hiding place for me; you preserve me from trouble; you surround me with shouts of deliverance. Selah.

Psalm 32:7

When I consider protection, I am reminded of the Prodigal Son and Elijah. As members of the body of Christ, we can, on occasion, bring a burden on ourselves, by behaving inappropriately. Likewise, we can be doing the will of God but be opposed by people and therefore placed in burdensome or dangerous situations. But God is faithful, despite our poor choices, or circumstances that are beyond our control, God still protects us.

We Might As Well Thank God Now

God is faithful. He does not go back on his Word.

If we are in trouble, he is right there in the thick of it, helping us navigate those areas with a confidence that relies on him.

We all know the story of the prodigal son, who wanted his inheritance early. After he squandered it away, he came back home to his father, head low and covered in shame. Rather than beat him up, his father threw a party in celebration. His father understood what God knows and attests, that we are all the more thankful to God for covering our sins when we know we don't deserve it. It is when we think higher of ourselves than we ought that God humbles us and helps us to see his sovereignty and that we are to choose holiness above all.

God is our refuge and strength, a
very present help in trouble.

Psalm 46:1

No Matter the Circumstance

Elijah did everything God told him to do. As a result, Jezebel, who was responsible for the murder of many of God's prophets, vowed to kill him as well. When

Elijah was at his weakest moment, God sent angels

to reaffirm him, strengthen him and direct him. God

protected him from his enemies and showed him that

there were many with him on the battlefield and that he

was not alone.

But You, O Lord, are a shield for me, my glory
and the One who lifts up my head.

Psalm 3:3

Giving It to Jesus

Some of life's most harrowing moments paralyze

us with fear. Especially when the result is because of a

mistake we made or the threats are asserted by someone

with so much power that fear is our most natural

response. Regardless of who is at fault, we can trust God

because he is faithful. Our role is to give it to him to

handle and let go of it.

For I am the Lord your God who takes hold of your
right hand and says to you, Do not fear; I will help you.

Isaiah 41:13

God's promise is to be with us at all times,

regardless of our choices or circumstance, God is our

protection.

Prayer

Most Gracious and Heavenly Father,

Thank you. Your presence shifts the atmosphere
and our recognition of your presence
provides security. Your love is greater than
any love we may receive from man.

For You bless the righteous, O Lord; You cover him
with favor as with a shield. (23) So we will not fear,
for you are with us; we will not be dismayed, for
you are our God. You will strengthen us and help
us; you will uphold us with your righteous right
hand. (24) You are my refuge and my shield; I have
put my hope in your word. (25) But let all who take
refuge in you be glad; let them ever sing for joy.
Spread your protection over them, that those who
love your name may rejoice in you. (26) May the
LORD answer you when you are in distress; may
the name of the God of Jacob protect you. (27)

In Jesus Name, Amen.

7

Character

But the fruit of the Spirit is love, joy, peace, forbearance, kindness, goodness, faithfulness, gentleness and self-control. Against such things there is no law.

Galatians 5:22-23

When we enter into a relationship with God, we become. The integrity and consistency of God's persistent character traits are adopted. We begin to reflect his light, love, and limitless possibilities.

God Teaches Us to Walk by Faith

God is everything he expects us to become and more. God is loving, kind, respectful, discreet, and authentic. He intimately shares unique details about our personal character traits and how we can shift our perspective and response to become all that he has created us to be. God positions us to learn valuable lessons so that in due season we are able to be what we desire and hope for. We can only do this through faith in God and not of ourselves.

We see this in the example of Jesus as he prepared to transition from his earthly state back into his heavenly state, he made sure his disciples were able to practice their faith with excellence. He teaches them the importance of "staying on the vine" (maintaining an intentional connection by forming a personal relationship with him) through the power of the Holy Spirit. In scripture, we see Jesus sending his disciples out, two by two, to preach the gospel with nothing to aid them but their faith in God. They suffered failures, persecution, and accusations from various community members along the way. Jesus showed the miracles afforded to those with faith, from feeding thousands with two fish and five loaves of bread, to calming a hurricane that had already killed many before their eyes.

For we walk by faith, not by sight.

2 Corinthians 5:5

God is Always Available and Pushing Us to Be More

Another character trait of God is that he is always available, listening, and responding in real time. We cannot always see him at work, but God never sleeps nor slumbers and his ways exceed our imagination, expectation, and determination. God pushes us into deep waters, but never allows them to overtake us.

Just as Jesus pushed his disciples to preach the gospel, heal the sick, and remain consistent under persecution - by power of the Holy Spirit, God is doing the same with each of us. We have been sent to do the will of God, to be his hands and feet, and to share his heart with others. This may mean sharing a message that is not well received or welcome at all. Regardless of the response we receive as we walk in our assignment, God is not surprised. In fact, God laughs at the enemy as he schemes because he knows his end from the beginning.

With this knowledge, we walk in faith, building our

character as we go safely beneath the shadow of God's

wing.

> *"Because he loves me," says the Lord, "I will rescue*
> *him; I will protect him, for he acknowledges my name.*
> *He will call on me, and I will answer him; I will be with*
> *him in trouble, I will deliver him and honor him. With*
> *long life I will satisfy him and show him my salvation."*
>
> *Psalm 91:14-16*

Light, Love and Limitless Possibility

Someone gave me a gift many years ago that

I cherish today. It reads, "Life is a canvas, paint it by

faith." Faith to do the will of God is a life of adventure.

You will look back on what God has done through your

obedience to his command and be amazed. We are

the bearers of light, when we enter the room we bring

something special with us and if we are doing it well, we

leave a piece of that with those we encounter to carry

forward.

The love God gives to us is unconditional. When we

walk in love, we learn to do the same. God will challenge

us in this area because it is a critical component of his character. It is what we all gravitate to when we have failed God, it is the magnet that attracts us to return and develop a deeper relationship.

When we walk in light and love, we open the door to endless possibility. Faith in God allows us to forgive, faith in God allows us to love in spite of our beliefs, faith in God allows us to persevere during trials, and it is our faith in God that pushes us beyond our personal goals into the stratosphere of God's plan.

> *"Very truly I tell you, whoever believes in me will do the works I have been doing, and they will do even greater things than these, because I am going to the Father. And I will do whatever you ask in my name, so that the Father may be glorified in the Son. You may ask me for anything in my name, and I will do it."*
>
> *John 14:12-14*

God's promise is to be with us at all times, as he develops our faith, directs our path, and opens doors no man can shut.

Prayer

Most Gracious and Heavenly Father.

Thank you. Your presence shifts the atmosphere
and our recognition of your presence
provides security. Your love is greater than
any love we may receive from man.

*If you are pleased with us, teach us your ways so we
may know you and continue to find favor with you.
Remember that this nation is your people. The Lord
replied, "My Presence will go with you, and I will
give you rest." (28) How will anyone know that you
are pleased with us and with your people unless
you go with us? What else will distinguish us from
all the other people on the face of the earth?" And
the Lord said (to Moses), "I will do the very thing you
have asked, because I am pleased with you and I
know you by name." Then 'we' (Moses) said, "Now
show us your glory." And the Lord said, "I will cause
all my goodness to pass in front of you, and I will
proclaim my name, the Lord, in your presence. I will
have mercy on whom I will have mercy, and I will have
compassion on whom I will have compassion. (29)*

In Jesus Name, Amen.

8

Greatness

*In the beginning was the Word, the Word was
with God, and the Word was God. He was with
God in the beginning. Through him all things
were made; without him nothing was made that
has been made. In him was life, and that life was
the light of all mankind. The light shines in the
darkness, and the darkness has not overcome it.*

John 1: 1-5

The Creator of All Things

Our recognition of God as the creator of all, Jesus

as the author and finisher of our faith, and the Holy

Spirit as our comforter, are the foundations by which the

believer stands.

The establishment of our faith begins with belief,

but is followed by confession and action. Without the

realization, recognition, and appropriate response to

what we believe, we are little more than bystanders.

Our mind, body, and soul are rooted and grounded in the structure of God's greatness and our heart rests in his power as the creator of all things. We love God with all of our hearts.

> One thing have I asked of the Lord, that will I seek
> after: that I may dwell in the house of the Lord
> all the days of my life, to gaze upon the beauty
> of the Lord and to inquire in his temple.
>
> Psalm 27:4

My God: Omnipresent, Omnibenevolent, Omniscient

God is always with us. God is love. God is all-knowing.

The calling upon God for help is a recurring theme throughout the Bible that is a reflection of relationship and trust. We see everyone from Moses to Jesus calls upon God daily for guidance, protection, provision, and help. More often than not, Jesus begins each of his prayers, thanking God.

Therefore, we too must follow suit and call upon him at all times. It doesn't matter if we simply whisper a small prayer under our breath, cry out to him in distress, sing to him in glee, or dance before him in praise - our personal relationship with God is what allows his greatness to be recognized in our lives. Others around us will wonder why or how we are who we are and it will be God's light shining through us.

A God who knows every hair that numbers my head, every situation that I will encounter before I experience it, who considers me worthy of his time or attention, is a God that deserves all of my praise, all of the glory, and the victory! He is my God. I may not always be what I should be, but he is always my God!

But for me it is good to be near God; I have made the Lord God my refuge, that I may tell of all your works.

Psalm 73:28

Abundance

God has all things.

When Moses and the children of Israel were walking in the dark running from Pharoah and his army

God was a cloud by day and fire by night. When Moses and the Israelites came upon the Red Sea, God parted the waters. When Elijah and Elisha were surrounded by the enemy, God blinded those who pursued them and revealed the army that was encamped around them in protection. When Joshua asked God to make the sun stand still so that they may complete the battle before them, the sun stood still. When Jesus needed money to pay his taxes, a fish swam up with a coin in his mouth. When Jesus needed a ride to the ceremony declaring his holiness and sovereignty, he appointed a donkey from the local neighborhood.

This is the God we serve, this is the God who loves us. Our confidence rests in him. He is abundant in love, abundant in mercy, abundant in presence. He surrounds us like a shield. We rest beneath the shadow of his wings. He prepares a space for us. He introduces new seasons, he brings blessings, favor, and everything we need, all in due season. He is intentional, thoughtful, thought-provoking and wonderful.

God is. Greatness comes with his presence.

And he said, "My presence will go with you, and I will give you rest."

Exodus 33:14

God's promise is to be with us at all times, and we rest in his greatness.

Prayer

Most Gracious and Heavenly Father,

Thank you. Your presence shifts the atmosphere and our recognition of your presence provides security. Your love is greater than any love we may receive from man.

I will exalt you, my God the King; I will praise your name for ever and ever. Every day I will praise you and extol your name for ever and ever. Great is the Lord and most worthy of praise; his greatness no one can fathom. One generation commends your works to another; they tell of your mighty acts. They speak of the glorious splendor of your majesty— and I will meditate on your wonderful works. They tell of the power of your awesome works—and I will proclaim your great deeds. They celebrate your abundant goodness and joyfully sing of your righteousness. The Lord is gracious and compassionate, slow to anger and rich in love. The Lord is good to all; he has compassion on all he has made. All your works praise you, Lord; your faithful people extol you. They tell of the glory of your kingdom and speak of your might, so that all people may know of your mighty acts and the glorious splendor of your kingdom. Your kingdom is an everlasting kingdom, and your dominion endures through all generations. The Lord is trustworthy in all he promises and faithful in all he does. The Lord upholds all who fall and lifts up all who are bowed down. The eyes of all look to you, and you give them their food at the proper time. You open your hand and satisfy the desires of every living thing. The Lord is righteous in all his ways and faithful in all he does. The Lord is near to all who call on him, to all who call on him in truth. He fulfills the desires of those who fear him; he hears their cry and saves them. The Lord watches over all who love him, but all the wicked he will destroy. My mouth will speak in praise of the Lord. Let every creature praise his holy name for ever and ever. (30)

In Jesus Name, Amen.

9

Sovereignty

Many are the plans in the mind of a man, but it is the purpose of the Lord that will stand.

Proverbs 19:21

Limitless Power

God has limitless power. Dominion belongs to him alone. God puts everything in order and rules with authority. While God has emotions, he does not act from a place of emotion. He is intentional. In his infinite wisdom, he formed all that exists - he incorporates systems within systems, seeds that generate seeds. He is The Great I am. He lives in each of us, moves through us, and rules in authority.

In the Book of Exodus, Pharaoh refused to let the people of Israel leave to worship God, he brought curses on the people of Egypt. But even greater, he brought a

terrible end for his own family. God sent the death angel

to kill the first born of every man and animal in Egypt

because of Pharaoh's unwillingness to acknowledge

God's authority and power.

> Not to us, Lord, not to us but to your name be the
> glory, because of your love and faithfulness. Why
> do the nations say, "Where is their God?" Our God
> is in heaven; he does whatever pleases him.
>
> Psalm 115:1-3

Reverence

In God's authority, he does not execute his power

without thought, concern or care for us. We may question

God, but we must do so in reverence to his power

and authority. Therefore, we must come before God in

humility. When we do, God answers us in his timing and

when we are truly ready to receive his answer.

Hannah was a barren woman who greatly desired

to have children. She would go to her church and pray

to God as she mourned her inability to bear children.

One day, as she prayed, the local pastor accused her of

being drunk, because her moans were so great. Hannah

took her issues to God and God alone. She did not broadcast them about the community, she communed with God and begged God to allow her to have children. God granted her request, and in appropriate response, Hannah birthed her son, taught him to worship, and dedicated his life to the Lord. Samuel, the prophet, an "arrow in the hand of God," lived a life of pure worship and dedication to God. Hannah was also granted more children.

> And we know that for those who love God
> all things work together for good, for those
> who are called according to his purpose.
>
> Romans 8:28

Infinite Wisdom & Godly Discernment

The wisdom of God will confuse and bewilder those who are wise in the way the world teaches us to be wise. Education provides a form of wisdom, but true wisdom comes from God. We do not gain access to this wisdom without a discerning spirit. This too comes from God. When we pray, we must ask God for wisdom and discernment as though they are twins born together from the womb. Why? Because wisdom without discernment is knowledge without a destination. We can have knowledge of a situation and even learn its most practical use and still not realize the true depth of our situation.

David was a young shepherd, minding his own business, worshipping God and doing as he was instructed. One day a prophet arrives at his family household and anoints him as king. David has no idea what this blessing may be or how he might achieve it but he receives it, despite his family only believing that the next anointed king would be handsome and tall like the previous king. In the Bible, it is very specific that God does not look at the outward appearance of the man, but at the heart of the man. When we look to God, and wait on his timing, and question his will or decision on a matter, we are walking beneath the sovereignty of God and he will have the final say.

The lot is cast into the lap, but its every
decision is from the Lord.

Proverbs 16:33

God's promise is to be with us at all times, his

sovereignty will reign.

Prayer

Most Gracious and Heavenly Father,

*Thank you. Your presence shifts the atmosphere
and our recognition of your presence
provides security. Your love is greater than
any love we may receive from man.*

*Yours, O Lord, is the greatness and the power and the
glory and the victory and the majesty, for all that is
in the heavens and in the earth is yours. Yours is the
kingdom, O Lord, and you are exalted as head above
all. Both riches and honor come from you, and you rule
over all. In your hand are power and might, and in your
hand it is to make great and to give strength to all. (31)*

*Fight the good fight of the faith. Take hold of the
eternal life to which you were called and about which
you made the good confession in the presence of
many witnesses. We are charged in the presence of
God, who gives life to all things, and of Christ Jesus,
who in his testimony before Pontius Pilate made
the good confession, to keep the commandment
unstained and free from reproach until the appearing
of our Lord Jesus Christ, which he will display at
the proper time—he who is the blessed and only
Sovereign, the King of kings and Lord of lords, who
alone has immortality, who dwells in unapproachable
light, whom no one has ever seen or can see.
To him be honor and eternal dominion. (32)*

In Jesus Name, Amen.

10

Power

*Trust in the Lord forever, for the Lord, the
Lord himself, is the Rock eternal.*

Isaiah 26:4

Amplification

Strength indicates the amount of force one may

have, but power is the ability to produce that strength

in an impressive amount of time. The presence of

power indicates the importance of a matter, a necessary

response that meets the moment.

When we call on God, he answers. In moments that

require immediate response, God's presence and power

are undeniable.

> *Now the Philistines had come and raided the Valley
> of Rephaim; so David inquired of God: "Shall I go and
> attack the Philistines? Will you deliver them into my
> hands?" The Lord answered him, "Go, I will deliver*

*them into your hands." So David and his men went up
to Baal Perazim, and there he defeated them. He said,
"As waters break out, God has broken out against my
enemies by my hand." So that place was called Baal
Perazim. The Philistines had abandoned their gods
there, and David gave orders to burn them in the fire.*

I Chronicles 14:9-12

Persuasion to Persist

God's power can persuade anyone to persist,
become, or act. God spoke to Abraham, Isaac, Jacob,
and Joseph prophesying futures they could not see, but
through faith in God's unconditional love and ability to
produce, they stayed their course.

It was God who gave Gideon the courage to defend
his faith. It was God who convinced the three Hebrew
boys that he had the power to save them no matter the
circumstance. It was God who appeared in a burning
bush to Moses. It was God who appeared as a cloud by
day, and fire by night, parted the Red Sea, and allowed
the water to flow from a rock in the wilderness. It was
God who gave Joseph a dream, Rahab hope, Deborah a
vision, and Ruth a new beginning.

Jesus turned the water into wine, caused a herd of pigs filled with demons to jump into the sea, commanded the storm of the sea to be still, brought Lazarus back to life, and healed the blind, lame, and those covered by leprosy. Jesus gave thanks to God and turned two fish and five loaves of bread into enough to feed thousands of people. Most importantly, Jesus saved all who acknowledge him as their Savior from a life of sin.

I can do all things through him who strengthens me.

Philippians 4:3

God's promise is to be with us at all times; His power is absolute.

Prayer

Most Gracious and Heavenly Father,

Thank you. Your presence shifts the atmosphere and our recognition of your presence provides security. Your love is greater than any love we may receive from man.

Behold, you have given us the authority to tread on serpents and scorpions, and over all the power of the enemy, and nothing shall hurt us. (33) For the kingdom of God does not consist in talk but in power. (34) But he said to me, "My grace is sufficient for you, for my power is made perfect in weakness." Therefore I will boast all the more gladly of my weaknesses, so that the power of Christ may rest upon me. (35) Being strengthened with all power, according to his glorious might, for all endurance and patience with joy. (36) So that our faith might not rest in the wisdom of men but in the power of God. (37)

In Jesus Name, Amen.

11

Miraculous

When Solomon had finished praying, fire came down from heaven and consumed the burnt offering and the sacrifices, and the [Shekinah] glory and brilliance of the Lord filled the house. The priests could not enter the house of the Lord because the glory and brilliance of the Lord had filled the Lord's house. When all the people of Israel saw how the fire came down and saw the glory and brilliance of the Lord upon the house, they bowed down on the stone pavement with their faces to the ground, and they worshiped and praised the Lord, saying, "For He is good, for His mercy and lovingkindness endure forever."

2 Chronicles 7:1-3

Shekinah Glory

The Shekinah Glory is "derived from the Hebrew root שָׁכַן (shakan), meaning "to dwell" or "to reside," the word "Shekinah" has long been understood in scholarly and traditional circles as symbolizing God's glory made visible and tangible." (38)

Therefore, the Shekinah Glory is the physical manifestation of God's presence among us, often in the form of atmospheric elements. When Moses asked God to "show me your glory" he had already experienced the presence of God in many ways: as a burning bush, as a pillar of cloud by day and fire by night, and as a cloud over the tent of meeting.

Moses created an atmosphere to spend time with God. He pitched a tent away from the camp of others, where everyone could witness him going to meet with God on a regular basis. When Moses would go to worship at the tent, not only would his aide Joshua be with him, but the people in the community would stand at their doors and worship as he communed there. It would also be obvious to the people that God was in the midst, as a cloud would cover the tent when Moses worshipped there.

> And the Lord said, "I will cause all my goodness to pass in front of you, and I will proclaim my name, the Lord, in your presence. I will have mercy on whom I will have mercy, and I will have compassion on whom

I will have compassion. But," he said, "you cannot see my face, for no one may see me and live."

Exodus 33:19-20

The Presence of the Lord is Here

There are moments in our lives when we can actually feel God's presence with us. We know God has ordained this moment to connect in a tangible way. In the Bible, when they recognized they were in the presence of God, a divine sense of awe, reverence, fear, and humility washed over them.

Moses worshipped God all of the time. He worshipped so often, that the people would see him enter the tent of meeting, and what proceeded was a cloud that would appear above the tent. Everyone went to stand in their doorways to worship God in those moments because it was obvious to all that God was meeting Moses in his time of prayer, meditation, and communion with God.

God's presence is felt most often when we are in sincere worship.

> *When Jesus saw Nathanael approaching,*
> *he said of him, "Here truly is an Israelite*
> *in whom there is no deceit."*
>
> *"How do you know me?" Nathanael asked.*
>
> *Jesus answered, "I saw you while you were still*
> *under the fig tree before Philip called you."*
>
> John 1:47-48

In the movie, 'The Gospel of John', this is one of my favorite scenes. In the scene, Nathanael remembers this moment of worship under the fig tree, and as he prays, a ray of sunlight peeks through the leaves and rests on him, as though God is responding to his prayer in worship. It was a special moment for Nathanael. When Jesus says this to Nathanael he knows that Jesus is indeed God and he is in awe.

The Miraculous

When the Shekinah Glory of the Lord appears, it is a strong indication God is moving in transformative ways.

When the manifestation of God came to Moses in a burning bush, it was because there was a dramatic shift about to happen in Moses' life.

When Joshua, the aide to Moses, would be in the tent of meeting worshipping with Moses, God was planting a seed in him. The people who witnessed the cloud descend upon the tent of meeting as they worshipped, witnessed the Shekinah Glory of God and they knew God was at work. (God knew he would take his people into the promised land, eventually. But in the interim, they had to learn to worship Him. Seeing Moses go to the mountain to worship and worship in the tent of meeting, taught them that God will meet them in worship.)

When Nathanael experienced the Shekinah Glory of God under the fig tree, he had no idea it would precede his coronation as a disciple under the tutelage of God himself manifest in Jesus Christ.

God's promise is to be with us at all times; but in seasons of remarkable transformation, he will manifest himself in the Shekinah Glory, the miraculous physical presence of God.

Prayer

Most Gracious and Heavenly Father,

Thank you. Your presence shifts the atmosphere
and our recognition of your presence
provides security. Your love is greater than
any love we may receive from man.

The Word became flesh and made His dwelling
among us. We have seen His glory, the glory of the
one and only Son from the Father, full of grace and
truth. (39) Out of his fullness we have all received
grace in place of grace already given. For the law
was given through Moses; grace and truth came
through Jesus Christ. (40) The Son is the radiance
of God's glory and the exact representation of his
being, sustaining all things by his powerful word.
After he had provided purification for sins, he sat
down at the right hand of the Majesty in heaven. (41)

In Jesus Name, Amen.

12

Tranquility

*He says, "Be still, and know that I am
God; I will be exalted among the nations,
I will be exalted in the earth."*

Psalm 46:10

Be Still

Sometimes, God just wants us to be still. Our

lives can pull us so many directions, but our tranquility

is connected to stillness in God. As I grew in my faith,

I realized a certainty, I must always stay connected to

God. Most mornings, I can sit and tarry with God. I make

time to hear from him (morning and evening) and to

reflect on what he is sharing with me. Today, he gave me

one word, tranquility.

Tranquility vs. Peace

I immediately thought, "Well Lord, we have already talked about how you bring peace." But I had to do some research. I found that there is a remarkable distinction between peace and tranquility.

Peace requires that certain conditions are met prior to obtaining it. Tranquility is available if we only be still. I have to admit, I have always felt little value for tranquility. I am someone who is always on the move. But tranquility allows for rest, reflection, and rejuvenation. The blessing often comes to those who are content, patient, and wait on God.

> *Saul waited there seven days for Samuel, as Samuel had instructed him earlier, but Samuel still didn't come. Saul realized that his troops were rapidly slipping away. So he demanded, "Bring me the burnt offering and the peace offerings!" And Saul sacrificed the burnt offering himself.*
>
> *Just as Saul was finishing with the burnt offering, Samuel arrived. Saul went out to meet and welcome him, but Samuel said, "What is this you have done?"*
>
> *Saul replied, "I saw my men scattering from me, and you didn't arrive when you said you would, and the Philistines are at Micmash ready for battle.*

So I said, 'The Philistines are ready to march against us at Gilgal, and I haven't even asked for the Lord's help!' So I felt compelled to offer the burnt offering myself before you came."

"How foolish!" Samuel exclaimed. "You have not kept the command the Lord your God gave you. Had you kept it, the Lord would have established your kingdom over Israel forever. But now your kingdom must end, for the Lord has sought out a man after his own heart. The Lord has already appointed him to be the leader of his people, because you have not kept the Lord's command."

I Samuel 13:8-14

The Value of Tranquility

One must choose tranquility and it requires intention. God so values tranquility that he made it one of the Ten Commandments. The Sabbath day is a day that is set aside for each of us to rest, reflect, and rejuvenate before God. It is a day that is ordained for intentional connection with God, without the worry of life.

Remember the Sabbath day by keeping it holy. Six days you shall labor and do all your work, but the seventh day is a sabbath to the Lord your God. On it you shall not do any work, neither you, nor your son or daughter, nor your male or female servant, nor your animals, nor any foreigner residing in your towns. For in six days the Lord made the heavens and the earth, the sea, and all that is in them, but

he rested on the seventh day. Therefore the Lord
blessed the Sabbath day and made it holy.

Exodus 20:8-11

A Man After God's Own Heart

Saul was unable to be still and it cost him the

kingdom. The prodigal son was unable to be still and it

cost him his inheritance. What are we sacrificing in our

efforts to achieve without acknowledging, appropriating,

or accepting the command of stillness with God? God

chose David because David could wait. He was content

with God's plan rather than trying to develop his own.

David wrote songs to God while he waited. David learned

to trust God while he waited. David learned the tone of

God's voice and to do his will while he waited.

Yet the Lord longs to be gracious to you; therefore
he will rise up to show you compassion. For the Lord
is a God of justice. Blessed are all who wait for him!

Isaiah 30:18

God's promise is to be with us at all times; but

stillness with God allows for sincere connection,

confidence, and contentment.

Prayer

Most Gracious and Heavenly Father.

Thank you. Your presence shifts the atmosphere and our recognition of your presence provides security. Your love is greater than any love we may receive from man.

But seek first the kingdom of God and his righteousness, and all these things will be added to you. (42) He leads the humble in what is right, and teaches the humble his way. (43) And we know that for those who love God all things work together for good, for those who are called according to his purpose. (44) For thus said the Lord God, the Holy One of Israel, "In returning and rest you shall be saved; in quietness and in trust shall be your strength." (45) Take my yoke upon you, and learn from me, for I am gentle and lowly in heart, and you will find rest for your souls. (46)

In Jesus Name, Amen.

13

Fortitude

*Jesus Christ is the same yesterday
and today and forever.*

Hebrews 13:8

The Mental Strength to Endure

God is with us in every moment we encounter. We

may feel alone, attacked, and angry - God knows. God

shares that His Strength is made perfect in weakness.

Attacks on our character, work ethic, aesthetic, or the

people we care for can hit us unexpectedly.

> *Korah son of Izhar, the son of Kohath, the son of Levi,
> and certain Reubenites—Dathan and Abiram, sons
> of Eliab, and On son of Peleth—became insolent and
> rose up against Moses. With them were 250 Israelite
> men, well-known community leaders who had been
> appointed members of the council. They came as a*

group to oppose Moses and Aaron and said to them, "You have gone too far! The whole community is holy, every one of them, and the Lord is with them. Why then do you set yourselves above the Lord's assembly?"

When Moses heard this, he fell facedown. Then he said to Korah and all his followers: "In the morning the Lord will show who belongs to him and who is holy, and he will have that person come near him. The man he chooses he will cause to come near him. You, Korah, and all your followers are to do this: Take censers and tomorrow put burning coals and incense in them before the Lord. The man the Lord chooses will be the one who is holy. You Levites have gone too far!"

Numbers 16:1-7

Our Response to Trouble

Pain, anger, and shame may be our first response to trouble, but it should not be our resolution. Our resolution must be rooted in the presence of God in that moment. God knows what we are facing and he hears the grumbling of those who are opposed to us. Instead of allowing our feelings to dictate our actions, we must instead allow our God to fight the battle for it belongs to him.

Moses did not appoint himself or his brother Aaron. God appointed them both - so the issue the community leaders had with Moses was not self-inflicted but more accurately an argument they had with God. We must learn as children of the Most High to let the Most High fight our battles, we have to learn to turn it over to Him.

When Korah had gathered all his followers in opposition to them at the entrance to the tent of meeting, the glory of the Lord appeared to the entire assembly. The Lord said to Moses and Aaron, "Separate yourselves from this assembly so I can put an end to them at once."

But Moses and Aaron fell facedown and cried out, "O God, the God who gives breath to all living things, will you be angry with the entire assembly when only one man sins?"

Then the Lord said to Moses, "Say to the assembly, 'Move away from the tents of Korah, Dathan and Abiram.'"

Moses got up and went to Dathan and Abiram, and the elders of Israel followed him. He warned the assembly, "Move back from the tents of these wicked men! Do not touch anything belonging to them, or you will be swept away because of all their sins." So they moved away from the tents of Korah, Dathan and Abiram. Dathan and Abiram had come

*out and were standing with their wives, children
and little ones at the entrances to their tents.*

*Then Moses said, "This is how you will know that the
Lord has sent me to do all these things and that it was
not my idea: If these men die a natural death and suffer
the fate of all mankind, then the Lord has not sent me.
But if the Lord brings about something totally new,
and the earth opens its mouth and swallows them, with
everything that belongs to them, and they go down
alive into the realm of the dead, then you will know
that these men have treated the Lord with contempt."*

*As soon as he finished saying all this, the ground under
them split apart and the earth opened its mouth and
swallowed them and their households, and all those
associated with Korah, together with their possessions.
They went down alive into the realm of the dead, with
everything they owned; the earth closed over them,
and they perished and were gone from the community.*

Numbers 16:19-31

God does not desire to hurt us. Moses spent so

much time with God that he began to care for people in

the same way that God does. He immediately prayed for

the people who might suffer needlessly. We see the same

reaction by Abraham when the Triune Godhead told him

they would destroy Sodom and Gomorrah.

Fortitude Precedes Forgiveness

God's presence not only allows us to have a mental strength to overcome adversity but being in His presence also gives us the ability to forgive those who hurt us. While the transition to forgiveness may be a harder lift and take time, it will come to those who bask in the presence of God. God forgives us daily for the sins we commit, who are we then to refuse forgiveness to those who offend or hurt us?

Jesus, our Savior, who never sinned was accused most of His adult life for blasphemy. He was beaten, spit on, talked about, and even put to death. The people chose to save a murderer's life rather than allow Jesus (the miracle worker) to live. But Jesus never sinned by cursing a man, harming a man, or even condemning a man. Instead, as men gambled for his clothing, stabbed him in his side, and gave him foul wine used to clean their private areas to drink, he asked God to forgive them.

*Jesus said, "Father, forgive them, for they
do not know what they are doing."*

Luke 23:34a

God is Consistent.
In His Presence – So Are We

With God, we are strong, resilient, protected, and guide by his presence. Nothing can prevent us from being accused, hurt, or the recipient of pain but by the will of God, we can respond with faith. We can turn it over to Him, prioritize compassion, and forgive those who hurt us.

*Then the Lord put out his hand and touched
my mouth. And the Lord said to me, "Behold,
I have put my words in your mouth.*

Jeremiah 1:9

God's promise is to be with us at all times; and in His presence he affords us fortitude and forgiveness to withstand any situation.

Prayer

Most Gracious and Heavenly Father,

*Thank you. Your presence shifts the atmosphere
and our recognition of your presence
provides security. Your love is greater than
any love we may receive from man.*

*For God gave us a spirit not of fear but of power and
love and self-control. (47) For by grace we have been
saved through faith. And this is not our own doing; it
is the gift of God, not a result of works, so that no one
may boast. (48) But the Lord God helps us; therefore
we have not been disgraced; therefore we have set
our face like a flint, and we know that we shall not
be put to shame. (49) But they who wait for the Lord
shall renew their strength; they shall mount up with
wings like eagles; they shall run and not be weary;
they shall walk and not faint. (50) For the Lord is slow
to anger and abounding in steadfast love, forgiving
iniquity and transgression, but he will by no means
clear the guilty, visiting the iniquity of the fathers on the
children, to the third and the fourth generation. (51)*

In Jesus Name, Amen.

14

Light

When Jesus spoke again to the people, he said, "I am the light of the world. Whoever follows me will never walk in darkness, but will have the light of life."

John 8:12

Righteousness and Justice

When we walk with God he shines a light on what is holy. God will also reveal what is unholy. There are times when God calls us to acknowledge the good or the ugly, and other times when he asks us to be still that he may fight the battle. Our responsive action is dictated through the prayer, the power of the Holy Spirit, and the illumination of his Word.

Righteousness and justice are the foundation of your throne; love and faithfulness go before you.

Blessed are those who have learned to acclaim
you, who walk in the light of your presence, Lord.

Psalm 89:14-15

Wisdom, Discernment and Revelation

The Spirit of the Lord is a gift that cannot be measured in material wealth, number of followers, or by the power of your influence. The Spirit of the Lord grants wisdom, discernment, and revelation. In the presence of God, we are forewarned of trouble before it occurs, we are certain of direction in the middle of a storm, and we are aware of what we should not be through the power of spiritual revelation.

Daniel, a young prophet in the Bible, was among many who claimed to reveal secrets when the king threatened to kill him and the other wise men if they could not reveal and interpret his dream. The king was angered when the magicians could not perform. But Daniel went to God and asked for a revelation.

*During the night the mystery was revealed
to Daniel in a vision. Then Daniel praised
the God of heaven and said:*

*"Praise be to the name of God for ever and ever;
wisdom and power are his. He changes times and
seasons; he deposes kings and raises up others.
He gives wisdom to the wise and knowledge to the
discerning. He reveals deep and hidden things; he
knows what lies in darkness, and light dwells with
him. I thank and praise you, God of my ancestors:
You have given me wisdom and power, you have
made known to me what we asked of you, you
have made known to us the dream of the king."*

Daniel 2:19-23

As Ambassadors of Christ, We are Called to Be the Light

When we walk with the Lord, there is not only
something that we should bring to every room we
enter, there is a part of us that we should also leave.
Our reverence, dependence, and communion with God
should be evident to all around us. We are to let our light
shine before others that they may glorify our Father in
heaven for our good works. This scripture means that our

light should bring a blessing into the room, a balm for

pained souls, a revelation for those who are lost, and a

protection or provision for those who need it.

> *For you were once darkness, but now you are*
> *light in the Lord. Live as children of light (for*
> *the fruit of the light consists in all goodness,*
> *righteousness and truth) and find out what pleases*
> *the Lord. Have nothing to do with the fruitless*
> *deeds of darkness, but rather expose them.*
>
> Ephesians 5:8-11

God's promise is to be with us at all times; and His

light illuminates all in its path bringing holiness, wisdom,

revelation and love.

Prayer

Most Gracious and Heavenly Father.

Thank you. Your presence shifts the atmosphere
and our recognition of your presence
provides security. Your love is greater than
any love we may receive from man.

So give your servant a discerning heart to govern your
people and to distinguish between right and wrong.

For who is able to govern this great people of yours? (52) For we know that whoever loves their brother and sister lives in the light, and in them there is no cause for stumbling. (53) And we have known and believed the love that God hath to us. God is love; and he that dwelleth in love dwelleth in God, and God in him. (54) Truly the light is sweet, and it is a pleasant thing for the eyes to see the sun. (55) The God of Israel said, the Rock of Israel spoke to me, 'One who rules over men righteously, who rules in the fear of God shall be as the light of the morning, when the sun rises, a morning without clouds, when the tender grass springs out of the earth, through clear shining after rain.' (56)

In Jesus Name, Amen.

15

Grace

*The Lord make his face to shine upon you
and be gracious to you; the Lord turn his
face toward you and give you peace.*

Numbers 6:25 - 26

Freedom

God grants us mercy each morning because we
need it. We are sinners. We were born that way. But God,
who is faithful, provided more than a promise with his
covenant, he gave of himself. He granted us the gift of
eternal life through Christ, his presence through the Holy
Spirit, and the ability to speak to Him one-on-one through
prayer, praise, and worship. This is the gift of freedom
through the presence of God.

But when they arrest you, do not worry about what to say or how to say it. At that time you will be given what to say, for it will not be you speaking, but the Spirit of your Father speaking through you. - Matthew 10:19

Favor

God's grace is unmerited favor. Grace is a gift that we could not earn. As an ambassador of Jesus Christ, we bring the presence of God everywhere that we go. God is light, love, peace, joy, sovereign, and wise. He is the beginning and the end, the creator of all things, in Him there is no division, he is faithful, consistent, and intentional. This is the oil we are covered in when we enter a space with the presence of God, favor is not simply attracted to us, favor is within us - like fire shut up in our bones. Our intentions, thoughts, actions, and words align with God granting us access to every blessing God has in store for us.

"Anyone who welcomes you welcomes me, and anyone who welcomes me welcomes the one who sent me. Whoever welcomes a prophet as a prophet will receive a prophet's reward, and whoever welcomes a righteous person as a righteous person will receive a righteous person's reward. And if

anyone gives even a cup of cold water to one of these little ones who is my disciple, truly I tell you, that person will certainly not lose their reward."

Matthew 10:40-42

Flawlessness

The grace of God's presence allows us to move freely and on purpose. The grace of God's presence eradicates fear and replaces it with bold confidence to pursue, endure, and succeed. We are not grasshoppers, we are conquerors who will be invited to the table of God, if we stay our course. We must invite the flawless nature of God to rest upon us that we may accomplish what he has assigned us to do. We each have a role and responsibility in the kingdom, but we cannot do it alone. We need the imperfect God to grant us his presence to go courageously forward into the destiny he has designed and planted as a desire within our hearts. The path is never straight, easy, or without agitation, but it is possible with God.

For a day in your courts is better than a thousand elsewhere. I would rather be a doorkeeper in the house of my God than dwell in the tents of wickedness. For the Lord God is a sun and shield;

the Lord bestows favor and honor. No good thing does he withhold from those who walk uprightly. O Lord of hosts, blessed is the one who trusts in you!

Psalm 84:10-12

God's promise is to be with us at all times; his presence grants us the freedom to be forgiven and to forgive, to be favored, and the fortitude to bring his flawless nature to any situation that we may accomplish his will.

Prayer

Most Gracious and Heavenly Father,

Thank you. Your presence shifts the atmosphere and our recognition of your presence provides security. Your love is greater than any love we may receive from man.

Hear me, Lord, and answer me, for I am poor and needy. Guard my life, for I am faithful to you; save your servant who trusts in you. You are my God; have mercy on me, Lord, for I call to you all day long. Bring joy to your servant, Lord, for I put my trust in you. You, Lord, are forgiving and good, abounding in love to all who call to you. Hear my prayer, Lord; listen to my cry for mercy. When I am in distress, I call to you, because you answer me. Among the gods there is none like you, Lord; no deeds can compare with yours. All the nations you have made will come and worship before you, Lord; they will bring glory to your name. For you are great and do marvelous deeds; you alone are God. Teach me your way, Lord, that I may rely on your faithfulness; give me an undivided heart, that I may fear your name. I will praise you, Lord my God, with all my heart; I will glorify your name forever. For great is your love toward me; you have delivered me from the depths, from the realm of the dead. Arrogant foes are attacking me, O God; ruthless people are trying to kill me–they have no regard for you. But you, Lord, are a compassionate and gracious God, slow to anger, abounding in love and faithfulness. Turn to me and have mercy on me; show your strength in behalf of your servant; save me, because I serve you just as my mother did. Give me a sign of your goodness, that my enemies may see it and be put to shame, for you, Lord, have helped me and comforted me. (57)

In Jesus Name, Amen.

16

Order

*For I know the plans I have for you, declares
the Lord, plans for welfare and not for evil,
to give you a future and a hope.*

Jeremiah 29:11

First Things First

This morning I awoke with work and business on my mind. Logically, I knew that addressing the many issues I faced at work and in my business before I communed, worshipped or spent time with God was a mistake that I honestly could not afford to make. Yet, still I struggled. I am distracted by my business at every turn but I know order is important. God's presence, his Holy Spirit reminds me that embracing the love, strength, confidence, peace, protection, character, greatness, sovereignty, power, miraculous nature, tranquility, fortitude, light and grace of God is my priority for many reasons. Our God is a jealous God because it is he who is our protection, provision, and our precision in every place and season. We are to love HIM with all of our hearts, minds, and souls.

> *Jesus replied: "'Love the Lord your God with all your heart and with all your soul and with all your mind.' This is the first and greatest commandment. And the second is like it: 'Love your neighbor as yourself.' All the Law and the Prophets hang on these two commandments."*
>
> Matthew 22:37-40

Systems
(The Fibonacci Spiral or the Golden Spiral)

God creates systems and systems are at the root of sustainability. God also creates chaos, chaos is at the root of disruption, and creativity sits at its feet. Which in turn, with proper reflection and intentionality, becomes a new system. It comes full circle. The seven day system that God created allows for reflection. God expects us to take a moment (on a regular basis) to stop and reflect, to watch and listen for God's voice and his intention. When

God created, he did so in six days, on the seventh he rested. After he created it he told us that what he created was good. Then on the seventh day, he rested and he told us to do the same. We are made in God's image.

In the Old Testament, we witness God as he observes his own actions and changes course. He did this in Genesis 6, when Noah found grace with God, and God flooded the earth. We see this again, when God regretted his decision to make Saul king and shifted to a man after his own heart. Again, we see this in his reflection of the law and his decision to be "God with Us" as Jesus Christ. Now we have the power of the Holy Spirit with each of us each day, bringing order out of chaos in our lives as we walk with Him.

God expects us to create systems and then to stop and reflect on our systems that we might make them better. If you look at an image of the Fibonacci spiral, (see below), it is like a winding staircase. It is a visual representation of reflection and knowledge, expansion and sustainability - which visually represents God's systemic order of operation. Designers use this model to create layouts (consider stages, theatres, advertisements, and movies) that are visually appealing to the mind's eye, because it correlates with God's design of our logic. Some people can see on this level with microscopic precision and speed while others may see this differently. Regardless, God is a God of order.

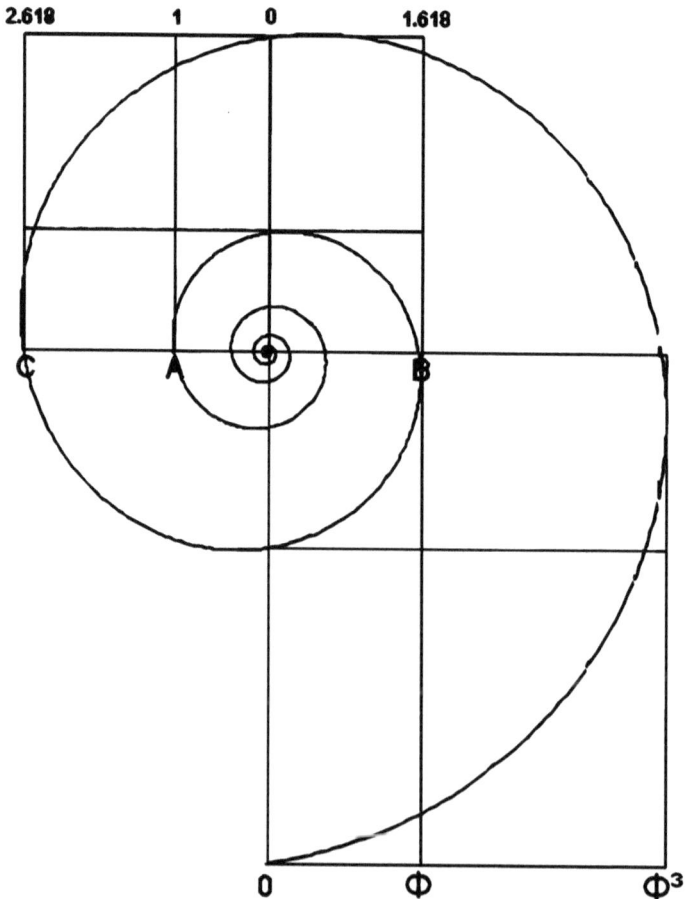

If any of you lacks wisdom, let him ask God, who gives generously to all without reproach, and it will be given him. But let him ask in faith, with no doubting, for the one who doubts is like a wave of the sea that is driven and tossed by the wind. For that person must not suppose that he will receive anything from the Lord; he is a double-minded man, unstable in all his ways.

James 1:5-8

Our Authority is God

God is the authority, he sets those in authority who he deems appropriate. It is our responsibility to respect those in authority and grant them the respect they deserve. We don't know what is ahead of us, but God does. He has a good plan for us, so those who are in authority are in authority for a reason. They may not always be good, but it will always work out for our good.

When we walk with God and confess and believe that Jesus is our Savior there are blessings that are afforded to us. We are in the presence of God. He tells us that vengeance belongs to Him and it is he who will repay. We need to move from a place of spiritual knowledge rather than our emotions. We need to understand that it is he who is with us and within us; he is greater than anyone in the world. Therefore, we can move in confidence, assured that our respect for authority is a reflection of our respect for God's order.

Yet, there are times when God calls us to stand 'out of order'. When Haman wanted Mordecai to bow to him like a God, he righteously refused. When Pharaoh ordered every male of the Israelites to be killed, the midwives refused. When Daniel was told not to pray openly or in public, he refused. When God tells you to do what is righteous, this is a Holy refusal. This is God's battle and he has assigned you as a warrior.

> *When Esther's words were reported to Mordecai, he sent back this answer: "Do not think that because you are in the king's house you alone of all the Jews will escape. For if you remain silent at this time, relief and deliverance for the Jews will arise from another place, but you and your father's family will perish. And who knows but that you have come to your royal position for such a time as this?"*
>
> *Esther 4:12-14*

God's promise is to be with us at all times; God's order is authoritative, systemic, disruptive, and reflective of his unending, unconditional, and unyielding love for us.

Prayer

Most Gracious and Heavenly Father,

Thank you. Your presence shifts the atmosphere and our recognition of your presence provides security. Your love is greater than any love we may receive from man.

We will trust in the Lord with all our heart, and will not lean on our own understanding. In all our ways we acknowledge you Lord, and you will make straight our paths. (59)

But because of his great love for us, God, who is rich in mercy, made us alive with Christ even when we were dead in transgressions—it is by grace we have been saved. And God raised us up with Christ and seated us with him in the heavenly realms in Christ Jesus, in order that in the coming ages he might show the incomparable riches of his grace, expressed in his kindness to us in Christ Jesus. For it is by grace we have been saved, through faith—and this is not from ourselves, it is the gift of God— not by works, so that no one can boast. For we are God's handiwork, created in Christ Jesus to do good works, which God prepared in advance for us to do. (59)

In Jesus Name, Amen.

17

Patience

Love is patient, love is kind. It does not envy, it does not boast, it is not proud.

I Corinthians 13:4

Excellence is Worth the Wait

God knows the end from the beginning, and while we do not know how our own specific stories will end, we know how it all ends. In the interim, we learn, experience, develop, and become. God's patience is love enacted through grace that waits with loving arms open and welcome for those who fall and fail over-and-over again. God is always available to listen and comfort to forgive and forget.

Who is a God like you, who pardons sin and forgives the transgression of the remnant of his inheritance? You do not stay angry forever but delight to show mercy. You will again have compassion on us; you will tread our sins underfoot and hurl all our iniquities into the depths of the sea. You will be faithful to Jacob, and show love to Abraham, as you pledged on oath to our ancestors in days long ago.

Micah 7:18-20

Endurance to Become

God grants us the endurance we need to become beautiful, ambassadors of Christ. For through the endurance of trial, the saving of our Savior, in times of arduous struggle, our humility is amplified, our gratitude exponential, and our walk becomes fortified. It is in this place that the rose grows from concrete.

Did you hear about the rose that grew from a crack in the concrete? Proving nature's law is wrong, it learned to walk without having feet. Funny it seems, but by keeping its dreams, it learned to breathe fresh air. Long live the rose that grew from concrete when no one else ever cared.

- Tupac Shakur (61)

It is in fact the patient presence of God that allows love to sprout and become in the most grotesque of places, it is the love of God, once allowed into our hearts, that waters those places in our hearts where it is dry and untouched, unseen by the light of day. Once we have experienced this type of love, it is difficult not to extend it. In fact, this is the purpose of patient endurance - that we might learn to love others as God first loved us.

Therefore, as God's chosen people, holy and dearly loved, clothe yourselves with compassion, kindness, humility, gentleness and patience. Bear with each other and forgive one another if any of you has a grievance against someone. Forgive as the Lord forgave you. And over all these virtues put on love, which binds them all together in perfect unity.

Colossians 3:12-14

God's promise is to be with us at all times; His patience develops us to reflect His likeness.

בטח *the* P R O M I S E
Prayer

Most Gracious and Heavenly Father,

Thank you. Your presence shifts the atmosphere and our recognition of your presence provides security. Your love is greater than any love we may receive from man.

Whatever we do, whether in word or deed, we do it all in the name of the Lord Jesus, giving thanks to God the Father through him. (62)

In Jesus Name, Amen.

18

Your Exceedingly Great Reward

*After this, the word of the Lord came to Abram
in a vision: "Do not be afraid, Abram. I am
your shield, your very great reward."*

Genesis 15:1

Nothing but the Blood

Jesus is at the center. When we are at our lowest,
God is there to create balance. God is aware of our
sadness, disappointments, and our situation. No matter
our effort, intention, dedication, or sacrifice, at times, our
reflection of life will tell us that we are simply not enough.
But the Holy Spirit is our intercessor. When we can't pray,
God prays.

In the same way, the Spirit helps us in our weakness.
We do not know what we ought to pray for, but the
Spirit himself intercedes for us through wordless
groans. And he who searches our hearts knows the
mind of the Spirit, because the Spirit intercedes
for God's people in accordance with the will of
God. And we know that in all things God works for
the good of those who love him, who have been
called according to his purpose. For those God
foreknew he also predestined to be conformed to
the image of his Son, that he might be the firstborn
among many brothers and sisters. And those he
predestined, he also called; those he called, he
also justified; those he justified, he also glorified.

What, then, shall we say in response to these things?
If God is for us, who can be against us? He who did
not spare his own Son, but gave him up for us all—how
will he not also, along with him, graciously give us all
things? Who will bring any charge against those whom
God has chosen? It is God who justifies. Who then is
the one who condemns? No one. Christ Jesus who
died—more than that, who was raised to life—is at the
right hand of God and is also interceding for us. Who
shall separate us from the love of Christ? Shall trouble
or hardship or persecution or famine or nakedness or
danger or sword? As it is written: "For your sake we
face death all day long; we are considered as sheep
to be slaughtered." No, in all these things we are
more than conquerors through him who loved us

Romans 8:26-37

God is Doing a New Thing

In the Bible, Abraham was faithful to God. He

worshipped him in wholeness and truth. He was blessed with an abundant life, and he gave God ten percent of all he had. He refused to take gifts from those who did not believe and trust in God. But he also desperately wanted a descendant to leave all that he earned and worked hard for to carry on his legacy.

God made Abraham a promise. He promised that he would have a descendant, many in fact. Abraham believed him. But as the years passed, his heart grew in sorrow. The promise God made him had yet to come to pass. In a fit of desperation, he took matters into his own hands. But that did not work out, instead it complicated his situation and set in motion a battle of nations (that would materialize many years later).

It was never Abraham's intention to go outside of the will of God, but when we wait for the promises of God, our hearts become tired and worn. In his pain, he hurt his wife and his wife's mistress to pursue his happiness.

*Hope deferred makes the heart sick, but
a longing fulfilled is a tree of life.*

Proverbs 13:12

It can be difficult to wait on God in seasons of unrest, pain, and disappointment. But we must hold on to the promise of God, to be with us during those seasons, even when we can't feel his presence.

"Remember not the former things, nor consider the things of old. Behold, I am doing a new thing; now it springs forth, do you not perceive it? I will make a way in the wilderness and rivers in the desert. The wild beasts will honor me, the jackals and the ostriches, for I give water in the wilderness, rivers in the desert, to give drink to my chosen people, the people whom I formed for myself that they might declare my praise."

Isaiah 43:18-21

Our Shield, Our Great Reward

Despite the mistakes of Abraham, God fulfilled his promise. He also protected Abraham from himself. When his mistress in her distress ran away, God comforted her and asked her to return and to submit to his wife (who hated her and her son). This allowed Abraham to experience the joy of having a descendant, while knowing that Ishmael (a living representation of Abraham's doubt) was not Isaac (the fulfillment of God's promise). In this, God granted Abraham a reprieve, a balm to comfort his pain, despite his disobedience.

God shielded Abraham with grace, forgiveness, and mercy.

God's promise is to be with us at all times; regardless of our failures, he is our shield and our greatest reward.

Prayer

Most Gracious and Heavenly Father,

Thank you. Your presence shifts the atmosphere and our recognition of your presence

provides security. Your love is greater than
any love we may receive from man.

But now thus says the Lord, he who created you, O
Jacob, he who formed you, O Israel: "Fear not, for I
have redeemed you; I have called you by name, you
are mine. When you pass through the waters, I will
be with you; and through the rivers, they shall not
overwhelm you; when you walk through fire you shall
not be burned, and the flame shall not consume you.
For I am the Lord your God, the Holy One of Israel, your
Savior. I give Egypt as your ransom, Cush and Seba
in exchange for you. Because you are precious in my
eyes, and honored, and I love you, I give men in return
for you, peoples in exchange for your life. Fear not, for
I am with you; I will bring your offspring from the east,
and from the west I will gather you. I will say to the
north, Give up, and to the south, Do not withhold; bring
my sons from afar and my daughters from the end of
the earth, everyone who is called by my name, whom
I created for my glory, whom I formed and made."

"Bring out the people who are blind, yet have eyes,
who are deaf, yet have ears! All the nations gather
together, and the peoples assemble. Who among
them can declare this, and show us the former
things? Let them bring their witnesses to prove
them right, and let them hear and say, It is true.

"You are my witnesses," declares the Lord, "and my
servant whom I have chosen, that you may know and
believe me and understand that I am he. Before me
no god was formed, nor shall there be any after me.
I, I am the Lord, and besides me there is no savior.
I declared and saved and proclaimed, when there
was no strange god among you; and you are my
witnesses," declares the Lord, "and I am God. Also

henceforth I am he; there is none who can deliver from my hand; I work, and who can turn it back?"

Thus says the Lord, your Redeemer, the Holy One of Israel: "For your sake I send to Babylon and bring them all down as fugitives, even the Chaldeans, in the ships in which they rejoice. I am the Lord, your Holy One, the Creator of Israel, your King."

Thus says the Lord, who makes a way in the sea, a path in the mighty waters, who brings forth chariot and horse, army and warrior; they lie down, they cannot rise, they are extinguished, quenched like a wick: "Remember not the former things, nor consider the things of old. Behold, I am doing a new thing; now it springs forth, do you not perceive it? I will make a way in the wilderness and rivers in the desert. The wild beasts will honor me, the jackals and the ostriches, for I give water in the wilderness, rivers in the desert, to give drink to my chosen people, the people whom I formed for myself that they might declare my praise." (63)

In Jesus Name, Amen.

19

Protection

"No one will be able to stand against you all the days of your life. As I was with Moses, so I will be with you; I will never leave you nor forsake you. Be strong and courageous, because you will lead these people to inherit the land I swore to their ancestors to give them.

"Be strong and very courageous. Be careful to obey all the law my servant Moses gave you; do not turn from it to the right or to the left, that you may be successful wherever you go. Keep this Book of the Law always on your lips; meditate on it day and night, so that you may be careful to do everything written in it. Then you will be prosperous and successful. Have I not commanded you? Be strong and courageous. Do not be afraid; do not be discouraged, for the Lord your God will be with you wherever you go."

Joshua 1:5-9

"*I Am*" with *You*

When Moses was challenged to return and save

his people, I can imagine his fear of returning to a place

where he'd murdered a man in a fit of rage. Not only was God asking him to return, God was asking him to save them.

When he was young, Moses was passionate about defending the rights of the Israelites. Though he was raised as an Egyptian, he'd discovered that when he was born he was adopted in an effort to save him from the slaughter of boys just like him. It was a miracle he was alive. He was raised in a palace, as a member of the royal family. But after he discovered his true identity, and witnessed the treatment of those who were born of the same culture, his anger rose each day. One day, it culminated in the murder of a man who spent his days berating and mistreating the Israelites. After Moses killed the man in front of so many witnesses, he ran to save his own life.

So, after many years, I can only imagine, Moses wondered why God would ask him, of all people, to return to this land and save his people. Moses was raised with the Pharaoh serving Egypt at that time and their reunion was not one Moses looked forward to. He'd grown immensely shy and stuttered when he spoke.

He was probably a shell of the man he was raised to be

due to the series of unfortunate events in his life. He was

satisfied to simply be a man, working the land, with a wife

and children.

> The Lord said, "I have indeed seen the misery of
> my people in Egypt. I have heard them crying out
> because of their slave drivers, and I am concerned
> about their suffering. So I have come down to rescue
> them from the hand of the Egyptians and to bring
> them up out of that land into a good and spacious
> land, a land flowing with milk and honey–the home of
> the Canaanites, Hittites, Amorites, Perizzites, Hivites
> and Jebusites. And now the cry of the Israelites has
> reached me, and I have seen the way the Egyptians
> are oppressing them. So now, go. I am sending you to
> Pharaoh to bring my people the Israelites out of Egypt."
>
> But Moses said to God, "Who am I that I should go
> to Pharaoh and bring the Israelites out of Egypt?"
>
> And God said, "I will be with you. And this will
> be the sign to you that it is I who have sent you:
> When you have brought the people out of Egypt,
> you will worship God on this mountain."
>
> Exodus 3:7-12

God Will Send Us to Do What Seems Impossible

God has been pushing me out of my comfort

zone this entire year. He's had me to stand on unfamiliar stages, to develop relationships at a deeper level leading to genuine friendships, to be an advocate for those in need, to lead a group of people who haven't had the opportunity to get to know, like, or trust me; to develop new skill sets and expand my horizon, and to stand as an ambassador among my peers for causes many would shudder to take on.

God even pushed me to ask for a promotion at work - probably the scariest thing I have done yet, because I cannot afford to lose the job I have but I also feel like I can't continue on in the way I have. I say he pushed me because I waited and waited and waited for the recognition to come, I worked hard and I gave my all (quite literally) to do the best job I could and no one said more than "thank you" and "good job." Don't get me wrong, words of affirmation are my love language, but working seven days a week, with the responsibilities I have can be overwhelming.

So here I am, learning, serving, and leading to be who God assigned me to be... but it is the scariest thing I have ever done.

God keeps telling me, "I am with you." So, I know, I am not alone. But there are moments when I feel like I am alone. When fear, imposter syndrome, nervousness, and anxiety develop roots - when disappointments, failures, and uncertainty creep into my psyche and whisper that I am not enough... In those moments, like Moses, or Gideon, or Elisha, I need God to show me a sign... to help me see Him at work in my life.

God's promise is to be with us at all times; he travels the same roads we travel and he knows every beat of our heart, we are at rest beneath the shadow of his wings.

Prayer

Most Gracious and Heavenly Father.

*Thank you. Your presence shifts the atmosphere
and our recognition of your presence
provides security. Your love is greater than
any love we may receive from man.*

*God is our refuge and strength, an ever-present help
in trouble. Therefore we will not fear, though the
earth gives way and the mountains fall into the heart*

of the sea, though its waters roar and foam and the mountains quake with their surging. There is a river whose streams make glad the city of God, the holy place where the Most High dwells. God is within her, she will not fall; God will help her at break of day. Nations are in uproar, kingdoms fall; he lifts his voice, the earth melts. The Lord Almighty is with us; the God of Jacob is our fortress. Come and see what the Lord has done, the desolations he has brought on the earth. He makes wars cease to the ends of the earth. He breaks the bow and shatters the spear; he burns the shields with fire. He says, "Be still, and know that I am God; I will be exalted among the nations, I will be exalted in the earth." The Lord Almighty is with us; the God of Jacob is our fortress. (64)

In Jesus Name, Amen.

20

Beneath the Shadow of His Wings

*God is our refuge and strength, a very present help
in trouble. Therefore will not we fear, though the
earth be removed, and though the mountains be
carried into the midst of the sea; Though the waters
thereof roar and be troubled, though the mountains
shake with the swelling thereof. Selah. There is a
river, the streams whereof shall make glad the city
of God, the holy place of the tabernacles of the
most High. God is in the midst of her; she shall not
be moved: God shall help her, and that right early.*

Psalm 46:1-5

Safe from Pursuit, Danger, or Trouble

God is our refuge, our safe space, from anything or

anyone who intends to harm or shame us. In the Hebrew,

this is referred to as Metzudah, which means refuge or

fortress. (65) The distinction and difference between

simply being protected and finding refuge is that a refuge is

a specific place, it is a fortress, it is being in the presence of

God. With God's presence he brings protection, but to be in

God, as one with God, we are in his secret place. He is our

hiding place, our fortress. No one can penetrate the shelter

of God.

When the angels of God went down to witness the

actions of those in Sodom and Gomorrah, Lot was waiting

at the gate of the town for travelers who innocently entered

the city's gate. In the evening, he begged them to stay with

him until the light of day, in an effort to protect them.

It all began when God heard the cries of Sodom and

Gomorrah.

> Then the Lord said, "The outcry against Sodom and
> Gomorrah is so great and their sin so grievous that I
> will go down and see if what they have done is as bad
> as the outcry that has reached me. If not, I will know."
>
> Genesis 18:20-21

> The two angels arrived at Sodom in the evening,
> and Lot was sitting in the gateway of the city. When
> he saw them, he got up to meet them and bowed
> down with his face to the ground. "My lords," he

*said, "please turn aside to your servant's house.
You can wash your feet and spend the night and
then go on your way early in the morning."*

*"No," they answered, "we will spend
the night in the square."*

*But he insisted so strongly that they did go with
him and entered his house. He prepared a meal
for them, baking bread without yeast, and they
ate. Before they had gone to bed, all the men from
every part of the city of Sodom—both young and
old—surrounded the house. They called to Lot, "Where
are the men who came to you tonight? Bring them
out to us so that we can have sex with them."*

Genesis 19:1-5

The danger that presented itself to any stranger

entering the town of Sodom and Gomorrah was insistent,

persistent, and incessant. It was the force of every man in

the city, there was a power dynamic so great that only a

man serving God could resist it. This is something that must

be acknowledged, this is the refuge of God's presence.

It is impenetrable. Lot walked with God and therefore he

remained the only man not subject to the evil that lay within

the men of Sodom and Gomorrah, he alone was safe from

harm. This is not something that we should walk by without

truly acknowledging that God is our refuge. The presence

of God was Lot's refuge. The presence of God is our refuge.

Don't think anyone or anything has power over God, we are

beneath the shadow of his wings.

> *"Get out of our way," they replied. "This fellow came*
> *here as a foreigner, and now he wants to play the*
> *judge! We'll treat you worse than them." They kept*
> *bringing pressure on Lot and moved forward to break*
> *down the door.*
>
> *But the men inside reached out and pulled Lot back*
> *into the house and shut the door. Then they struck the*
> *men who were at the door of the house, young and old,*
> *with blindness so that they could not find the door.*
>
> *The two men said to Lot, "Do you have anyone else*
> *here—sons-in-law, sons or daughters, or anyone*
> *else in the city who belongs to you? Get them*
> *out of here, because we are going to destroy this*
> *place. The outcry to the Lord against its people*
> *is so great that he has sent us to destroy it."*
>
> *Genesis 19:10-13*

Not only will God protect you, he will confuse and

destroy your enemies so that you will have a safe way of

escape.

A Secure Place to Find Rest and Peace

As the apple of God's eye, the intimacy we

experience with him is often strengthened by the

consistency of his presence, especially in times of potential hurt, harm, or danger. The love he has for us is exemplified in the love we have for him, and his desire to protect us in our most vulnerable state is an experience we can truly have with no other. For God's protection does not come in the same form as man's protection, it is all-encompassing, and impenetrable.

> Therefore Jesus said again, "Very truly I tell you,
> I am the gate for the sheep. All who have come
> before me are thieves and robbers, but the sheep
> have not listened to them. I am the gate; whoever
> enters through me will be saved. They will come
> in and go out, and find pasture. The thief comes
> only to steal and kill and destroy; I have come
> that they may have life, and have it to the full.
>
> John 10:7-10

David was an innocent shepherd who worshipped God and was anointed to be king. David was enveloped in God's presence, his worship allowed him to not only be protected but also to become the protector of many through skilled warriorship. David was often pursued and his enemies came in many forms, from those who cared for him to those he cared for - no matter who pursued

David, God was his fortress.

God's promise is to be with us at all times; he is our impenetrable safe space.

Prayer

Most Gracious and Heavenly Father,

Thank you. Your presence shifts the atmosphere and our recognition of your presence provides security. Your love is greater than any love we may receive from man.

David sang to the Lord the words of this song when the Lord delivered him from the hand of all his enemies and from the hand of Saul. He said: "The Lord is my rock, my fortress and my deliverer; my God is my rock, in whom I take refuge, my shield and the horn of my salvation.

He is my stronghold, my refuge and my savior—from violent people you save me.

"I called to the Lord, who is worthy of praise, and have been saved from my enemies. The waves of death swirled about me; the torrents of destruction overwhelmed me. The cords of the grave coiled around me; the snares of death confronted me.

"In my distress I called to the Lord; I called out to my God. From his temple he heard my voice; my cry came to his ears. The earth trembled and quaked, the foundations of the heavens shook; they trembled because he was angry. Smoke rose from his nostrils; consuming fire came from his mouth, burning coals blazed out of it. He parted the heavens and came

down; dark clouds were under his feet. He mounted the cherubim and flew; he soared on the wings of the wind. He made darkness his canopy around him—the dark rain clouds of the sky. Out of the brightness of his presence bolts of lightning blazed forth. The Lord thundered from heaven; the voice of the Most High resounded. He shot his arrows and scattered the enemy, with great bolts of lightning he routed them. The valleys of the sea were exposed and the foundations of the earth laid bare at the rebuke of the Lord, at the blast of breath from his nostrils.

"He reached down from on high and took hold of me; he drew me out of deep waters. He rescued me from my powerful enemy, from my foes, who were too strong for me. They confronted me in the day of my disaster, but the Lord was my support. He brought me out into a spacious place; he rescued me because he delighted in me.

"The Lord has dealt with me according to my righteousness; according to the cleanness of my hands he has rewarded me. For I have kept the ways of the Lord; I am not guilty of turning from my God. All his laws are before me; I have not turned away from his decrees. I have been blameless before him and have kept myself from sin. The Lord has rewarded me according to my righteousness, according to my cleanness in his sight.
"To the faithful you show yourself faithful, to the blameless you show yourself blameless, to the pure you show yourself pure, but to the devious you show yourself shrewd. You save the humble, but your eyes are on the haughty to bring them low. You, Lord, are my lamp; the Lord turns my darkness into light. With your help I can advance against a troop; with my God I can scale a wall.

"As for God, his way is perfect: The Lord's word is flawless; he shields all who take refuge in him. For who is God besides the Lord? And who is the Rock except

our God? It is God who arms me with strength and keeps my way secure. He makes my feet like the feet of a deer; he causes me to stand on the heights. He trains my hands for battle; my arms can bend a bow of bronze. You make your saving help my shield; your help has made me great. You provide a broad path for my feet, so that my ankles do not give way.

"I pursued my enemies and crushed them; I did not turn back till they were destroyed. I crushed them completely, and they could not rise; they fell beneath my feet. You armed me with strength for battle; you humbled my adversaries before me. You made my enemies turn their backs in flight, and I destroyed my foes. They cried for help, but there was no one to save them—to the Lord, but he did not answer. I beat them as fine as the dust of the earth; I pounded and trampled them like mud in the streets.

"You have delivered me from the attacks of the peoples; you have preserved me as the head of nations. People I did not know now serve me, foreigners cower before me; as soon as they ear of me, they obey me. They all lose heart; they come trembling from their strongholds.

"The Lord lives! Praise be to my Rock! Exalted be my God, the Rock, my Savior! He is the God who avenges me, who puts the nations under me, who sets me free from my enemies. You exalted me above my foes; from a violent man you rescued me. Therefore I will praise you, Lord, among the nations; I will sing the praises of your name.

"He gives his king great victories; he shows unfailing kindness to his anointed, to David and his descendants forever." (66)

In Jesus Name, Amen.

21

The Solution

For in this hope we were saved. But hope that is seen is no hope at all. Who hopes for what they already have? But if we hope for what we do not yet have, we wait for it patiently. In the same way, the Spirit helps us in our weakness. We do not know what we ought to pray for, but the Spirit himself intercedes for us through wordless groans. And he who searches our hearts knows the mind of the Spirit, because the Spirit intercedes for God's people in accordance with the will of God. And we know that in all things God works for the good of those who love him, who have been called according to his purpose.

Romans 8:24-28

Problems

God recognizes that many are suffering, either through actual outcries or simply by the pleading of their hearts. God appeared in many places where people were hurting without their request for his presence.

Abraham asked his wife to pretend to be his sister as they travelled, subjecting her to the wiles of those in leadership to ensure his safety. While she agreed to do so, I can only imagine this broke her heart.

Now Abraham moved on from there into the region of the Negev and lived between Kadesh and Shur. For a while he stayed in Gerar, and there Abraham said of his wife Sarah, "She is my sister." Then Abimelek king of Gerar sent for Sarah and took her. But God came to Abimelek in a dream one night and said to him, "You are as good as dead because of the woman you have taken; she is a married woman."

—-

Abraham replied, "I said to myself, 'There is surely no fear of God in this place, and they will kill me because of my wife.' Besides, she really is my sister, the daughter of my father though not of my mother; and she became my wife. And when God had me wander from my father's household, I said to her, 'This is how you can show your love to me: Everywhere we go, say of me, "He is my brother."

Then Abimelek brought sheep and cattle and male and female slaves and gave them to Abraham, and he returned Sarah his wife to him. And Abimelek said, "My land is before you; live wherever you like." To Sarah he said, "I am giving your brother a thousand shekels of silver. This is to cover the offense against you before all who are with you; you are completely vindicated."

Genesis 20:1-3, 11–16

Theories of Solution

Sin is pervasive, as it permeated and exponentially

took over the cities of Sodom and Gomorrah, and

Nineveh, at one point it also encompassed the entire

world. We can witness how God approached this in the

Old Testament, and the executed power of the New

Covenant.

The Lord saw how great the wickedness of the human race had become on the earth, and that every inclination of the thoughts of the human heart was only evil all the time. The Lord regretted that he had made human beings on the earth, and his heart was deeply troubled. So the Lord said, "I will wipe from the face of the earth the human race I have created—and with them the animals, the birds and the creatures that move along the ground—for I regret that I have made them."

But Noah found favor in the eyes of the Lord.

Genesis 6:5-8

In the Old Testament, God would destroy areas

that were infested with sin, like Sodom and Gomorrah

and eventually the entire world, he left only a seed of life

(Noah and those with him) to begin again. Noah found

favor because he walked with God at the center of his

heart. This recognition of a solution, led God to a theory

of becoming "God with Us."

We see this executed through his sojourning with

Abraham, Isaac, Joseph, Moses and Joshua (with each of

them, he appeared as the Shekinah Glory). We see it as

he spoke through the prophets, over and over again. We

see it as God called David, a man after his own heart.

Testing His Hypothesis

That which was from the beginning, which we have

heard, which we have seen with our eyes, which we have

looked at and our hands have touched—this we proclaim

concerning the Word of life. The life appeared; we have

seen it and testify to it, and we proclaim to you the eternal

life, which was with the Father and has appeared to us.

We proclaim to you what we have seen and heard, so that

you also may have fellowship with us. And our fellowship is with the Father and with his Son, Jesus Christ. We write this to make our joy complete. - I John 1:1-4

Jesus was sent as a man, the human physical manifestation of "God with Us." Jesus was known as a miracle worker, a great teacher, the lover of all, we could look at Jesus and see that we were indeed made in the image of God. When Jesus came as a man in physical form, his church was created.

Let's reflect on the beginning of creation, with every development, God told himself, "It was good." I can only imagine how he identified the problem, developed his theory, and tested his hypothesis that he recognized - it was good.

Execution of His Solution

God within us.

"All this I have spoken while still with you. But the Advocate, the Holy Spirit, whom the Father will send in my name, will teach you all things and will remind you of everything I have said to you.

Peace I leave with you; my peace I give you. I do not give to you as the world gives. Do not let your hearts be troubled and do not be afraid."

John 14:25-27

Our Living is Not in Vain

God hears the pleading of our hearts, he sees the tears we shed in secret places, and he hears our cries of despair. We are not alone. God is with us. God sees and he knows and he is balancing every scale, justice and vengeance are in his hands. We need only be still and see the salvation of the Lord.

God knew when Tamar was raped by her brother, when Gideon considered God as he gathered wheat from the threshing floor, when a man filled with demons suffered alone in a cave locked away in chains, and when a woman with the issue of blood would fight through a crowd to simply touch his hem. God knows He hears us, he feels our pain, and he is acutely aware of our circumstances.

God's promise is to be with us at all times; his presence is our solution.

Prayer

Most Gracious and Heavenly Father,

Thank you. Your presence shifts the atmosphere and our recognition of your presence provides security. Your love is greater than any love we may receive from man.

May the Spirit of the Lord rest upon us, the Spirit of wisdom and understanding, the Spirit of counsel and might, the Spirit of knowledge and the fear of the Lord. (67) "If you love me, you will keep my commandments. And I will ask the Father, and he will give you another Helper, to be with you forever, even the Spirit of truth, whom the world cannot receive, because it neither sees him nor knows him. You know him, for he dwells with you and will be in you." (68) Now the Lord is the Spirit, and where the Spirit of the Lord is, there is freedom. (69) May the God of hope fill you with all joy and peace in believing, so that by the power of the Holy Spirit you may abound in hope. (70) And hope does not put us to shame, because God's love has been poured into our hearts through the Holy Spirit who has been given to us. (71)

In Jesus Name, Amen.

22

Rest

Come to me, all who labor and are heavy laden, and I will give you rest. Take my yoke upon you, and learn from me, for I am gentle and lowly in heart, and you will find rest for your souls. For my yoke is easy, and my burden is light."

Matthew 11:28-30

An Unhurried Rhythm

It can be difficult to find rest when you are burdened with responsibilities and the litigious list of tasks are required in order to survive. Addictions tend to fall upon us at our worst moments, becoming a workaholic is no different. When life is a constant whirl of chaos and you feel a tremendous responsibility to do all that you can to ride the wave, you do exactly that but the wave may not stop for days, weeks, months or years. But the rest that God's presence brings presents an unhurried

rhythm, one that dictates when to move and when to be.

Moses had become a trusted leader among the

Israelites due to his knowledge on the will of God, and his

relationship with God. They elected him to be their judge

to settle disputes. But Moses was called to do this day

and night and he was tired, extremely tired. His father-in-

law, Jethro, came to visit and challenged his decision to

serve in this way.

Moses' father-in-law said to him, "What you are doing is not good. You and the people with you will certainly wear yourselves out, for the thing is too heavy for you. You are not able to do it alone. Now obey my voice; I will give you advice, and God be with you! You shall represent the people before God and bring their cases to God, and you shall warn them about the statutes and the laws, and make them know the way in which they must walk and what they must do. Moreover, look for able men from all the people, men who fear God, who are trustworthy and hate a bribe, and place such men over the people as chiefs of thousands, of hundreds, of fifties, and of tens. And let them judge the people at all times. Every great matter they shall bring to you, but any small matter they shall decide themselves. So it will be easier for you, and they will bear the burden with you. If you do this, God will direct you, you will be able to endure, and all this people also will go to their place in peace."

So Moses listened to the voice of his father-in-law
and did all that he had said. - Exodus 18:17-24

Quiet Confidence

We don't have to solve every problem or do

everything. As a single mother raised by a single mother,

it is hard to 'lay your burdens down.' I was always taught

that there is no one coming to save you. You must do

all that you can to survive, grit, tooth, and nail. Fight

for what you want and 'tell it like it is' because closed

mouths don't get fed. As a result, I have been known

to be vocal, passionate, hard-working, productive, and

efficient. I learned to develop workflows so that systems

could replace the chaos that inefficiency brings when so

much is placed upon your shoulders. As single mothers,

we were forced to be resilient, forced to be strong, but it

wasn't pleasant to watch or experience.

Therefore thus says the Holy One of Israel, "Because
you despise this word and trust in oppression and
perverseness and rely on them, therefore this iniquity
shall be to you like a breach in a high wall, bulging
out and about to collapse, whose breaking comes
suddenly, in an instant; and its breaking is like that of a
potter's vessel that is smashed so ruthlessly that among

its fragments not a shard is found with which to take fire from the hearth, or to dip up water out of the cistern."

For thus said the Lord God, the Holy One of Israel, "In returning and rest you shall be saved; in quietness and in trust shall be your strength."

Exodus 30:12-15

We cannot allow our logic to supersede what we know intimately about God, that He is faithful and he will see us through. We have permission to let go, rest, and give it to him.

Therefore the Lord waits to be gracious to you, and therefore he exalts himself to show mercy to you. For the Lord is a God of justice; blessed are all those who wait for him.

Exodus 30:18

Leading the Way

We will be burdened, there is no doubt. We will have work to do. We will have to submit to authority and look to the hills. But God, who is faithful, will never leave us nor forsake us. He is going to be right there with us at every moment. We must keep our minds on him in order to maintain our peace. God desires to be good to us, to replenish us, and to direct us.

For a people shall dwell in Zion, in Jerusalem; you shall weep no more. He will surely be gracious to you at the sound of your cry. As soon as he hears it, he answers you. And though the Lord give you the bread of adversity and the water of affliction, yet your Teacher will not hide himself anymore, but your eyes shall see your Teacher. And your ears shall hear a word behind you, saying, "This is the way, walk in it," when you turn to the right or when you turn to the left.

Isaiah 30:19-21

A Beautiful Sound

When we rest, we pray and praise God because it is easier to recognize Him at work in our lives. When we take a moment to reflect upon all that has happened we see God moving in a wonderful and mighty way. When we let go, the joy in our heart is given permission to resonate and enjoy the beauty of life. This is our praise, our joy, our wonderment, excitement and the gift of God.

God's promise is to be with us at all times; we can rest and give it all to him.

Prayer

Most Gracious and Heavenly Father,

Thank you. Your presence shifts the atmosphere
and our recognition of your presence
provides security. Your love is greater than
any love we may receive from man.

O Lord, my heart is not lifted up; my eyes are not raised
too high; I do not occupy myself with things too great
and too marvelous for me. But I have calmed and
quieted my soul, like a weaned child with its mother;
like a weaned child is my soul within me. O Israel, hope
in the Lord from this time forth and forevermore. (72)

In Jesus Name, Amen.

23

Joy

Then Nehemiah the governor, Ezra the priest and teacher of the Law, and the Levites who were instructing the people said to them all, "This day is holy to the Lord your God. Do not mourn or weep." For all the people had been weeping as they listened to the words of the Law.

Nehemiah said, "Go and enjoy choice food and sweet drinks, and send some to those who have nothing prepared. This day is holy to our Lord. Do not grieve, for the joy of the Lord is your strength."

The Levites calmed all the people, saying, "Be still, for this is a holy day. Do not grieve."

Then all the people went away to eat and drink, to send portions of food and to celebrate with great joy, because they now understood the words that had been made known to them.

Nehemiah 8:9-12

Getting to Know Him

The revelation of Jesus Christ awarded to us as individuals opens an intimacy with God that allows us to connect with him in magnificent ways. We begin to study and seek God in a way that is authentic. Our pursuit of God, our thirst for God, is what brings him joy and when God is pleased with how we experience and appreciate his presence, it is his joy that gives us strength.

"If you remain in me and my words remain in you, ask whatever you wish, an it will be done for you. This is to my Father's glory, that you bear much fruit, showing yourselves to be my disciples.

"As the Father has loved me, so have I loved you. Now remain in my love. If you keep my commands, you will remain in my love, just as I have kept my Father's commands and remain in his love. I have told you this so that my joy may be in you and that your joy may be complete. My command is this: Love each other as I have loved you. Greater love has no one than this: to lay down one's life for one's friends. You are my friends if you do what I command. I no longer call you servants, because a servant does not know his master's business. Instead, I have called you friends, for everything that I learned from my Father I have made known to you. You did not choose me, but I chose you and appointed you so that you

might go and bear fruit–fruit that will last–and so that whatever you ask in my name the Father will give you. This is my command: Love each other.

John 15:7-17

Joy is Expressed Love for Others

Nothing makes me happier than to see my mother happy. My brother, sister, and I were raised by a woman that was strong, hard-working, loving and secure in her trust of Jesus Christ as her Savior. She showed us through her actions that she was willing to give all of herself that we might live wonderful and amazing lives. She did her absolute best to raise us as confident, intelligent, respectful individuals who would contribute more than we took, love more than we argued, and be more than we shrank. This is no simple feat. The strength of a single mother with limited income is to endure with grace, fortitude and strength - a strength that can only come with faith, prayer, and praise.

Our lives are an expression of her love for us. Much like my mother, Jesus sacrificed his life for each of us, and the lives we have the freedom to live are expressions of his love for us.

Our grace afforded through the sacrifice of his life is what gives us strength to forgive others, but more importantly, ourselves. Mercy anew each morning helps us to return to God, asking his forgiveness, mercy, and grace to walk with Him one more time. It deepens our intimacy with God.

> *You make known to me the path of life; in your presence there is fullness of joy; at your right hand are pleasures forevermore.*
>
> Psalm 16:11

Fruit that Will Last

In my life, I have been granted many blessings. Opportunities I never imagined have been presented to me, some I was prepared for, others maybe not. Nonetheless, God granted me access. Of all that he has allowed, I can see the fruit that will remain.

I prayed for many years that God would make me a perfect conduit of his message and his love. Perfection is in Christ, if I am in Him and He is in me, I am able to be what God has placed in my heart as a sincere desire.

Opportunities arise, and if God says go, I go and be whatever it is He wants me to be in that moment. As a result, doors have opened for me that I could never imagine. God has granted me joy in simply being everything he has created me to be, nothing more and nothing less.

> *Go, eat your bread with joy, and drink your wine with a merry heart, for God has already approved what you do.*
>
> *Ecclesiastes 9:7*

God's promise is to be with us at all times; in his presence is the fullness of joy.

Prayer

Most Gracious and Heavenly Father.

Thank you. Your presence shifts the atmosphere and our recognition of your presence provides security. Your love is greater than any love we may receive from man.

Give praise to the Lord, proclaim his name; make known among the nations what he has done. Sing to him, sing praise to him; tell of all his wonderful acts. Glory in his holy name; let the hearts of those who seek the Lord rejoice. Look to the Lord and his strength; seek his face always. Remember the wonders he has done, his miracles, and the judgments he pronounced, you his servants, the descendants of Israel, his chosen ones, the children of Jacob. He is the Lord our God; his judgments are in all the earth.

He remembers his covenant forever, the promise he made, for a thousand generations, the covenant he made with Abraham, the oath he swore to Isaac. He confirmed it to Jacob as a decree, to Israel as an everlasting covenant: "To you I will give the land of Canaan as the portion you will inherit."

When they were but few in number, few indeed, and strangers in it, they wandered from nation to nation, from one kingdom to another. He allowed no one to oppress them; for their sake he rebuked kings: "Do not touch my anointed ones; do my prophets no harm."

Sing to the Lord, all the earth; proclaim his salvation day after day. Declare his glory among the nations, his marvelous deeds among all peoples. For great is the Lord and most worthy of praise; he is to be feared above all gods. For all the gods of the nations are idols, but the Lord made the heavens. Splendor and majesty are before him; strength and joy are in his dwelling place. (73)

In Jesus Name, Amen.

24

Elevation

"The kingdom of heaven is like treasure hidden in a field, which a man found and covered up. Then in his joy he goes and sells all that he has and buys that field."

Matthew 13:44

Perspective

The presence of God shifts how we see situations we are placed in, it shifts the narrative, and invites a delightful ending to a matter that was once filled with chaos, sadness, and pain. Our lives on earth can be full of trouble - even when we dedicate our lives to God. This is why the world is constantly trying to convince others that walking with the Lord is of no effect, but how wrong they are. Their lack of awareness and discernment renders them incapable of guiding you to a place of understanding. God is omnipresent, omnibenevolent, and omniscient. He sees, he knows, and he cares. His love is not just for us and our pain is sometimes meant to bless others, that they too may find Christ and be healed.

Oh, the depth of the riches and wisdom and knowledge of God! How unsearchable are his judgments and how inscrutable his ways!

Romans 11:33

Favor, Authority, and Honor

When we can walk in the will of God, forsaking what we think should be, we will begin to walk on purpose. Our alignment, peace, and acceptance of the communication, navigation, and destination accelerates our elevation. God's greatest desire is to bless us, but our unwillingness to obey, to seek him, and to listen for his direction may have us fighting battles in the wilderness because we are not readying ourselves for war. When we take the time to keep God first, he will be right there at our side telling us which way to go and what steps to take. When we try to take our own route, we stumble and we fall and if we are not careful, that fall can be great. But when we are ready, like David, God will shine a light on us, anoint us, and

position us for seats of favor, authority, and honor.

Therefore, preparing your minds for action, and being
sober-minded, set your hope fully on the grace that
will be brought to you at the revelation of Jesus Christ.
As obedient children, do not be conformed to the
passions of your former ignorance, but as he who
called you is holy, you also be holy in all your conduct.

I Peter 1:13-15

Our Faith, His Glory

Trusting God is at the center of elevation. We

cannot see it but we know it. We trust his whisper. We

know he is going before us to make every crooked place

straight. We believe that God is for us and not against

you. Faith not only guides us, it gives us zeal, earnestness,

and a clear path to take. We cannot imagine how pleased

God is when he experiences our trust. We know that we

trust him when we praise him at every moment, no matter

what it looks like - we know our blessing is on the way.

And without faith it is impossible to please
God, because anyone who comes to him

*must believe that he exists and that he
rewards those who earnestly seek him.*

Hebrews 11:6

God's promise is to be with us at all times; elevation
is available to those who seek, trust, and obey.

Prayer

Most Gracious and Heavenly Father,

*Thank you. Your presence shifts the atmosphere
and our recognition of your presence
provides security. Your love is greater than
any love we may receive from man.*

*We praise you, God, we praise you, for your Name
is near; people tell of your wonderful deeds. You
say, "I choose the appointed time; it is I who judge
with equity. When the earth and all its people
quake, it is I who hold its pillars firm. To the
arrogant I say, 'Boast no more,' and to the wicked,
'Do not lift up your horns. Do not lift your horns
against heaven; do not speak so defiantly.'"*

*No one from the east or the west or from the desert
can exalt themselves. It is God who judges: He
brings one down, he exalts another. In the hand
of the Lord is a cup full of foaming wine mixed*

with spices; he pours it out, and all the wicked of the earth drink it down to its very dregs.

As for me, I will declare this forever; I will sing praise to the God of Jacob, who says, "I will cut off the horns of all the wicked, but the horns of the righteous will be lifted up." (74)

In Jesus Name, Amen.

25

Access

One thing have I asked of the Lord, that will I seek after: that I may dwell in the house of the Lord all the days of my life, to gaze upon the beauty of the Lord and to inquire in his temple.

Psalm 27:4

In God's Presence We Experience the Absence of Fear

When we are truly in the presence of God, we will not experience fear. We will consider our situations and choose to replace fear with faith in God, and therefore, build confidence in spaces when we question the intentions of others. We know that no matter what happens, God is with us. So whether we stand or fall, are safe or are harmed, we know our outcome is to be with

Our Heavenly Father, who loves us dearly. We also know that God is for us. Because we seek God, and walk with God, and consider the will of God, we can know that he is with us and our actions have led us to a situation in which God will get the glory. This was the power behind the three Hebrew boys in the fiery furnace, Daniel in the Lion's Den, and David on the run from his predecessor, Saul.

> *But for me it is good to be near God; I have made the Lord God my refuge, that I may tell of all your works.*
>
> Psalm 73:28

Dwell

Chase God. Desire God. Seek God.

The comfort and love that comes from just being in His presence, is exponentially greater than being in the presence of the family member who loves and dotes on us the most, or the spouse that is consistently present, available, and trustworthy. God's love is so good, that we can become addicted to its opiate effect of euphoria.

When we realize that the God who created the heavens

and the earth, is right here with us, and that he knows

us - every pain in our heart, every ache in our belly, and

every tear that we cry, we want to be with Him. We love

spending time with people who truly know us and we

hate to disappoint them. We want them to see us, hear us,

and speak to us.

> *You have said, "Seek my face." My heart says*
> *to you, "Your face, Lord, do I seek."*
>
> *Psalm 27:8*

Gaze

Have you ever found yourself gazing at something

for longer than you felt you should? Perhaps it is a

beautiful person, a picturesque landscape, or an

elaborate painting. No matter what it is you are gazing

upon, you feel in your heart you are seeing something

magnificent or wonderful and your physical body cannot

deviate from what your heart is saying when it witnesses

this beauty first-hand. This should be our reaction to

Jesus Christ, when we witness the Holy Spirit at work, or realize the depth of love God has for us. We should be in awe of the intentionality, specificity, and intimacy of God. God has orchestrated a beautiful life that we have the opportunity to live because we have direct access to God. Those who lived before us, before Christ's sacrifice and before the gift of the Holy Spirit had a different encounter with God. God was always present, but we did not always realize we had direct access to Him. Jesus had to reveal that to his disciples, but those who worshipped God in wholeness and truth before the birth of Jesus Christ were aware. Abraham sat in the presence of God. Moses sat in the presence of God. David sat in the presence of God. Each with their own personal encounter with God, gazed upon his beauty and in awe, responded with fellowship, love, appreciation, and trust.

"Blessed are the pure in heart, for they shall see God."

Matthew 5:8

Inquire

Ask God.

When we trust God, we ask him for help because we know that God is faithful. We know that God loves us and through his love, we receive forgiveness, mercy, and grace. We know that the Lord is our shepherd, and we trust His guidance. When we know that God is with us telling us which way to go and how to make good decisions, we trust Him enough to ask for help. When we have walked with God for a season, we know that he alone is our help.

For he will hide me in his shelter in the day of trouble; he will conceal me under the cover of his tent; he will lift me high upon a rock. And now my head shall be lifted up above my enemies all around me, and I will offer in his tent sacrifices with shouts of joy; I will sing and make melody to the Lord. Hear, O Lord, when I cry aloud; be gracious to me and answer me! - Psalm 27:5-7

God's promise is to be with us at all times; therefore

we have been granted access to the unyielding gift of His

presence.

Prayer

Most Gracious and Heavenly Father,

*Thank you. Your presence shifts the atmosphere
and our recognition of your presence
provides security. Your love is greater than
any love we may receive from man.*

*The Lord is my shepherd; I shall not want. He
makes me lie down in green pastures. He leads
me beside still waters. He restores my soul. He
leads me in paths of righteousness for his name's
sake. Even though I walk through the valley of the
shadow of death, I will fear no evil, for you are with
me; your rod and your staff, they comfort me.*

*You prepare a table before me in the presence
of my enemies; you anoint my head with oil;
my cup overflows. Surely goodness and mercy
hall follow me all the days of my life, and I shall
dwell in the house of the Lord forever. (75)*

In Jesus Name, Amen.

26

Wellness

I am the Lord who heals you.

Exodus 15:26

God is Our Healer

Jesus often healed the sick in miraculous ways.
The presence of the Lord is able to heal any sickness we
may suffer from. We must call on Him, and only believe.
The woman with the issue of blood heard many stories
about Jesus, so when he was near she did all she could to
simply touch the hem of his garment to be made whole.
Another mother, whose child was possessed by demons
and sick, met Jesus and his disciples at dinner. When
Jesus met her, he told her in his own way that his healing

was entitled to the Jews, as God's chosen people. She in turn, replied to him that even the dogs get to eat the crumbs from the master's table, which impressed Jesus and he healed her daughter.

While today, love and fellowship with Christ is available to every man, there may be many among us who do not worship and feel they are not entitled to God's healing, love, mercy, or grace. It is up to us to believe and share our beliefs with others that God is a healer and no respecter of persons. The same healing we receive anyone who submits their life to Christ is entitled to. For none of us deserve it, it is the gift of God.

Then they cried to the Lord in their trouble, and He saved them from their distress. He sent out His word and healed them; He rescued them from the grave.

Psalm 107:19-20

God Relieves Our Anxiety

God does not want us to walk around stressed out about potential outcomes and scenarios. Instead, in faith, we are to trust him and know that God is in control and the battle we face belongs to him. While it can be difficult to quiet our fears, our anxious minds, God ensures us that if we keep pointing that anxiety back to him, and keep our mind on what he promises, we can ease our minds. We just have to confess, know, and believe that God is for us and that he desires to bless us. Even when things that we worry about come to pass, we must know that God has a better plan.

Joseph was betrayed by his brothers, sold into slavery and believed by his father to be left dead with only a blood-stained coat to remember him by. The broken hearts of Joseph and his father were heartbeats God heard every day and every night until they were both restored to God's intended destinations. After much hardship and trouble, Joseph was blessed beyond belief and able to save those who betrayed him and be reunited with his father. God always had a plan. If Joseph only focused on his condition instead of God's revealed intention for his life, he would have never made it to be second in command to the king. God gave him a vision at a young age, and rather than allow the enemy to roar as loud as a lion, placing obstacle after obstacle in his way, he held onto his dreams.

Humble yourselves, therefore, under God's mighty hand, so that in due time He may exalt you. Cast all your anxiety on Him, because He cares for you. Be sober-minded and alert. Your adversary the devil prowls around like a roaring lion, seeking someone to devour.

I Peter 5:6-8

Jesus Defeated Death and the Grave

When it is all said and done, God has the final say. Jesus sacrificed his life so that we may have eternal life. Whether we live here on earth or pass away into the by and by - God is with us. We are always going to be in the presence of God and God will always care for us. It is what he has done since the beginning of time and what he will always do. We can give God praise and thank him for his gracious gift that we could never deserve.

Praise the Lord, my soul, and forget not all his benefits—
who forgives all your sins and heals all your diseases.

Psalm 103:2-3

God's promise is to be with us at all times; in his

presence we are healed, protected, and safe.

Prayer

Most Gracious and Heavenly Father,

Thank you. Your presence shifts the atmosphere
and our recognition of your presence
provides security. Your love is greater than
any love we may receive from man.

Rejoice in the Lord always; again I will say,
rejoice. Let your reasonableness be known to
everyone. The Lord is at hand; do not be anxious
about anything, but in everything by prayer and
supplication with thanksgiving let your requests
be made known to God. And the peace of God,
which surpasses all understanding, will guard
your hearts and your minds in Christ Jesus.

Finally, brothers, whatever is true, whatever is
honorable, whatever is just, whatever is pure, whatever

is lovely, whatever is commendable, if there is any excellence, if there is anything worthy of praise, think about these things. What you have learned and received and heard and seen in me–practice these things, and the God of peace will be with you. (76)

Have you not known? Have you not heard? The Lord is the everlasting God, the Creator of the ends of the earth. He does not faint or grow weary; his understanding is unsearchable. He gives power to the faint, and to him who has no might he increases strength. Even youths shall faint and be weary, and young men shall fall exhausted; but they who wait for the Lord shall renew their strength; they shall mount up with wings like eagles; they shall run and not be weary; they shall walk and not faint. (77)

In Jesus Name, Amen.

27

Mercy

The steadfast love of the Lord never ceases; his mercies never come to an end; they are new every morning; great is your faithfulness.

Lamentations 3:22-23

Merciful God

Amazing grace! How sweet the sound, That saved a wretch; like me! I once was lost, but now am found. Was blind, but now I see.

John Newton (78)

There is nothing like the grace of God that can be found anywhere else, it is a grace that often we aren't willing to even extend to ourselves. As I began to write this devotional, I considered my own sins of gluttony,

selfishness, envy, and more. Sins that at times, I condemn

myself for because how can I, someone who loves God

so much, still find myself wallowing in sin? Is my belief

and confession a lie, I certainly hope not. As my greatest

fear is to be found unworthy of God's presence when it is

all said and done. It would break my heart.

I imagine that David, a man who spent his entire life

worshipping God, felt the same way. He truly loved God.

David looked to God for guidance and protection.

*And Samuel said to Saul, "You have done foolishly. You
have not kept the command of the Lord your God, with
which he commanded you. For then the Lord would
have established your kingdom over Israel forever. But
now your kingdom shall not continue. The Lord has
sought out a man after his own heart, and the Lord has
commanded him to be prince over his people, because
you have not kept what the Lord commanded you.*

I Samuel 13·14

God Recognizes Our Love for Him

Just as God chose David over Saul, God chooses

those whose hearts are aligned with His. He wants us

to desire to do His will above our own. We may sin, but overall, our goals and our intentions align with the will of God. David was not a perfect man. In fact, we can go through the Bible and count his sins. Sin did not negate God's love for David. David loved God. This I believe is what was missing from Saul. Saul was transactional - he did what the prophet told him to do because he believed it gave him position, power, and prominence. His intentions were to uplevel and become more, they had nothing to do with God. David on the other hand, loved God, he praised God, wrote songs to God, and he truly worshiped God in wholeness and spirit.

Psalm 116, entitled, "I love the Lord" is a letter of devotion, gratitude, and awe of God penned by David long ago and it encapsulates his love for God. God is near to those who truly love him despite their sin.

I do not understand what I do. For what I want to do I do not do, but what I hate I do. And if I do what I do not want to do, I agree that the law is good. As it is, it is no longer I myself who do it, but it is sin living in me. For I know that good itself does not dwell in me, that is, in my sinful nature. For I have the desire to do what is good, but I cannot carry it out. For I do not do the good I want to do, but the evil I do not want to do—this I keep on doing. Now if I do what I do not want to do, it is no longer I who do it, but it is sin living in me that does it.

Romans 7:15-20

Sin Carries the Distinction that We are Human and God is Divine

Only Jesus can walk the earth as a human and not sin, because he was divine. Only the Holy Trinity has the ability to forgive sin. It is the nature of our beings to sin. God always grants us a way of escape, but our human nature is revealed every time we choose to go another route.

God is always with us, he sees us, he knows us, and he will never leave nor forsake us. For this, we can give him praise!

He has told you, O man, what is good; and what does the Lord require of you but to do justice, and to love kindness, and to walk humbly with your God? - Micah 6:8

God's promise is to be with us at all times; by his stripes we are healed from the nature of our sin, for he is with us in every moment.

Prayer

Most Gracious and Heavenly Father,

Thank you. Your presence shifts the atmosphere and our recognition of your presence provides security. Your love is greater than any love we may receive from man.

This is the message we have heard from him and proclaim to you, that God is light, and in him is no darkness at all. If we say we have fellowship with him while we walk in darkness, we lie and do not practice the truth. But if we walk in the light, as he is in the light, we have fellowship with one another, and the blood of Jesus his Son cleanses us from all sin. If we say we have no sin, we deceive ourselves, and the truth is not in us. If we confess our sins, he is faithful and just to forgive us our sins and to cleanse us from all unrighteousness. If we say we have not sinned, we make him a liar, and his word is not in us. (79)

Gracious is the Lord, and righteous; our God is merciful. The Lord preserves the simple; when I was brought low, he saved me. Return, O my soul, to your rest; for the Lord has dealt bountifully with you. For you have delivered my soul from death, my eyes from tears, my feet from stumbling; I will walk before the Lord in the land of the living. (80)

In Jesus Name, Amen.

28

Truth

"If you love me, keep my commands. And I will ask the Father, and he will give you another advocate to help you and be with you forever—the Spirit of truth. The world cannot accept him, because it neither sees him nor knows him. But you know him, for he lives with you and will be in you. I will not leave you as orphans; I will come to you. Before long, the world will not see me anymore, but you will see me. Because I live, you also will live. On that day you will realize that I am in my Father, and you are in me, and I am in you. Whoever has my commands and keeps them is the one who loves me. The one who loves me will be loved by my Father, and I too will love them and show myself to them."

John 14:15-21

The Only Way

The presence of God reminds us of who we are.

We are His and we are ambassadors of Christ. God

shows his love for us by remaining in truth; he is faithful

and will always do what he promises to do. As we were made in his likeness, our love toward him should also be consistent. Jesus asks us as believers to keep his commands, to walk in alignment with his will, and according to his way.

It is not difficult to obey God, we just make it seem like it is. We often want sin and God, but God wants us to choose - are we going to walk in truth or walk in sin?

"And you will know the truth, and the truth will set you free."

John 8:32

The Truth Guides Us

For those of us who love God, it is our greatest desire to make our home with Him. In order to do so, we must be in the will of God. This may not be difficult to do, but at times, we may make the wrong choice. The Holy Spirit, gifted to us, through the sacrifice of Jesus that he might be God within us, helps us to recognize those bad choices before they happen. God is faithful, he always offers us a way of escape. Jesus is our escape and he is

faithful to forgive our sins, once we confess them and

repent.

> *"I am the vine; you are the branches. If you remain in me and I in you, you will bear much fruit; apart from me you can do nothing. If you do not remain in me, you are like a branch that is thrown away and withers; such branches are picked up, thrown into the fire and burned. If you remain in me and my words remain in you, ask whatever you wish, and it will be done for you. This is to my Father's glory, that you bear much fruit, showing yourselves to be my disciples."*

John 15:5-8

Always Working to Help Us Understand Who He Is

Being in the presence of God exposes us to one

consistent heartbeat, God loves us and desires to be

with us at all times. Much like a parent's love, God loves

is unconditional - his actions coincide with his promises.

Every day that we awake, we have been blessed with

another opportunity to appreciate God's presence

and his love. But this only happens when we try our

best to get to know Him in wholeness and truth. When

we seek Him and his guidance, when we thirst for the

comprehensive, all-knowing, soul-searching, faithful

and good love that only God can provide. God makes

himself available at every moment to help us understand

this in a myriad of ways. Even at the end, Jesus wanted

us to understand who he was so that we may better

understand who we are.

"You are a king, then!" said Pilate.

Jesus answered, "You say that I am a king. In fact, the
reason I was born and came into the world is to testify
to the truth. Everyone on the side of truth listens to me."

John 18:37

Love is patient and kind; love does not envy or boast;
it is not arrogant or rude. It does not insist on its
own way; it is not irritable or resentful; it does not
rejoice at wrongdoing, but rejoices with the truth.

I Corinthians 13:4-6

God's promise is to be with us at all times; as he

guides us in truth.

Prayer

Most Gracious and Heavenly Father,

Thank you. Your presence shifts the atmosphere
and our recognition of your presence
provides security. Your love is greater than
any love we may receive from man.

To the lady chosen by God and to her children,
whom I love in the truth—and not I only, but also
all who know the truth—because of the truth,
which lives in us and will be with us forever:

Grace, mercy and peace from God the
Father and from Jesus Christ, the Father's
Son, will be with us in truth and love.

It has given me great joy to find some of your children
walking in the truth, just as the Father commanded
us. And now, dear lady, I am not writing you a new
command but one we have had from the beginning.
I ask that we love one another. And this is love: that
we walk in obedience to his commands. (81)

In Jesus Name, Amen.

בטח *the* P R O M I S E

29

The Name of Jesus

*Therefore God exalted him to the highest place
and gave him the name that is above every name,
that at the name of Jesus every knee should bow,
in heaven and on earth and under the earth.*

Philippians 2:9-10

Authority

When we call on the name of Jesus Christ, we are

asking God to not only be present but to come with his

full authority, we are invoking the sovereignty of God in a

situation. God's authority is limitless, boundless, infinite,

and all powerful. When the blind man Bartimaeus sat by

the roadside begging and heard that Jesus was passing

by, he screamed, "Jesus, Son of David, have mercy on

me!" (82) He cried in recognition that this was his chance,

his one opportunity, to have Jesus heal him from the

weight of disability.

> *The name of the Lord is a fortified tower;*
> *the righteous run to it and are safe.*

Proverbs 18:10

United in Mind and Thought

The body of Jesus Christ agrees that Jesus is Lord of Lords and Kings of Kings. Our confession of such is what unites us as one. We are able to touch and agree that Jesus is Lord, therefore we are bound together as one body, working our gifts as God has ordained each of us to do. As we worship the Lord individually, we worship collectively, walking lock in step with the will of God and each other. Even when arguments or disagreements arise, our foundation is sure, we call on the name of Jesus, who is our Savior, and ruler over all.

> *I appeal to you, brothers and sisters, in the*
> *name of our Lord Jesus Christ, that all of you*
> *agree with one another in what you say and that*
> *there be no divisions among you, but that you*
> *be perfectly united in mind and thought.*

I Corinthians 1:10

Righteousness

We could be as 'holy' as the Sanhedrins or the Jews who murdered Jesus on the cross and never be seen as righteous before God, because our righteousness rests in Jesus Christ alone. It is he who washes us clean and presents us as holy before his Father. We have no ability to do this on our own because it is in our nature to sin. Therefore, only by the Power of the Holy Spirit and the Blood of Jesus Christ are we able to overcome the sin of this world. When we call on the name of Jesus, demons flee. It is the name of Jesus that convicts without condemnation. It is the name of Jesus that saves us. He is our righteousness.

*The Lord is my shepherd, I lack nothing. He makes
me lie down in green pastures, he leads me beside
quiet waters, he refreshes my soul. He guides
me along the right paths for his name's sake.*

Psalm 23:1-3

God's promise is to be with us at all times; in his presence is the authority, unity, and righteousness that

בטח *the* P R O M I S E ————————

comes in the Name of Jesus.

Prayer

Most Gracious and Heavenly Father,

*Thank you. Your presence shifts the atmosphere
and our recognition of your presence
provides security. Your love is greater than
any love we may receive from man.*

*Not to us, Lord, not to us but to your name be
the glory, because of your love and faithfulness.
Why do the nations say, "Where is their God?"*

*Our God is in heaven; he does whatever pleases
him. But their idols are silver and gold, made by
human hands. They have mouths, but cannot speak,
eyes, but cannot see. They have ears, but cannot
hear, noses, but cannot smell. They have hands, but
cannot feel, feet, but cannot walk, nor can they utter
a sound with their throats. Those who make them
will be like them, and so will all who trust in them.*

*All you Israelites, trust in the Lord—he is their help
and shield. House of Aaron, trust in the Lord—he*

*is their help and shield. You who fear him, trust
in the Lord—he is their help and shield.*

*The Lord remembers us and will bless us: He will bless
his people Israel, he will bless the house of Aaron, he
will bless those who fear the Lord—small and great alike.*

*May the Lord cause you to flourish, both you
and your children. May you be blessed by
the Lord, the Maker of heaven and earth.*

*The highest heavens belong to the Lord, but the earth
he has given to mankind. It is not the dead who praise
the Lord, those who go down to the place of silence; it*

is we who extol the Lord, both now and forevermore.

Praise the Lord.(83)

In Jesus Name, Amen.

30

Redemption

I will restore to you the years that the swarming locust has eaten, the hopper, the destroyer, and the cutter, my great army, which I sent among you. "You shall eat in plenty and be satisfied, and praise the name of the Lord your God, who has dealt wondrously with you. And my people shall never again be put to shame.

Joel 2:25-26

Restoring What Was Lost

The Lord thunders at the head of his army; his forces are beyond number, and mighty is the army that obeys his command. The day of the Lord is great; it is dreadful. Who can endure it?

Joel 2:11

The Day of the Lord is closer than we think.

The Lord will come with his great army and all that

we know and recognize as 'life' will cease. But God, in his graciousness, offers a way of escape to each of us - repentance. If we repent and return to God, he will restore all that was lost. We are the children of God and he loves us unconditionally, but he gives us the freedom to choose. When we choose to walk with Him, and choose His way, forgiveness, abundance, peace and rest are available to us as non-negotiable blessings.

> *"Even now," declares the Lord, "return to me*
> *with all your heart, with fasting and weeping and*
> *mourning." Rend your heart and not your garments.*
> *Return to the Lord your God, for he is gracious*
> *and compassionate, slow to anger and abounding*
> *in love, and he relents from sending calamity.*
>
> Joel 2:12-13

Making All Things Possible

When we walk with God, things we have hoped for, that we may have believed were impossible become possible. After many years of hope, Abraham and Sarah in the Bible were able to have a child. Joshua, deep in battle, was able to make time stand still… and the mother of Moses was able to save her son despite the obstacles

WALK BOLDLY WITH GOD

that threatened him with death.

I can remember when I'd fumbled as a college
student, ambitiously adding more classes than my
financial aid could pay for and was forced to stop going
to school. I was derailed for 4 to 5 years, paying what I
owed a little at a time. It broke my heart and when I was
finally done paying my debt, my entire degree program
had changed. I would have to give another four years to
get my Bachelors degree. I cried in hopelessness and
desperation to God. Then an advisor called me and told
me she'd made a way for me to finish in 12 months, and
that I could walk the stage in 6 months. I will never ever
forget that day. God made the impossible possible for
me. As a single parent, this meant the world to me. I
wanted to show my children that they could go back to
school and become whatever they hoped to become. I
also showed them that God was making a way for me,
that it wasn't just me, it was my faith, my worship, and

God himself who made the difference.

Return to your stronghold, O prisoners of hope;
today I declare that I will restore to you double.

Zechariah 9:12

Savior

The Lord, who is present in every moment, sees

our tears. He understands why we choose to sin, why

we walk in anxious wonder, praying to see a solution to

our problems. He knows every enemy, and he laughs at

their plans, while we worry and stress. God, who desires

that we turn every concern over to Him, is standing at the

door waiting on us to simply let Him in. Jesus, who is with

us, the Holy Spirit which is within each of us, and God as

the triune head are available and waiting to allow us to let

them in. We must be willing to let go and let God handle

what hurts us, what pains us, what worries us and what

consumes us.

The thief comes only to steal and kill and destroy. I came that they may have life and have it abundantly.

John 10:10

God's promise is to be with us at all times; he brings redemption to restore, heal, and save.

Prayer

Most Gracious and Heavenly Father,

Thank you. Your presence shifts the atmosphere and our recognition of your presence provides security. Your love is greater than any love we may receive from man.

I will extol the Lord at all times; his praise will always be on my lips. I will glory in the Lord; let the afflicted hear and rejoice. Glorify the Lord with me; let us exalt his name together. I sought the Lord, and he answered me; he delivered me from all my fears. Those who look to him are radiant; their faces are never covered with shame. This poor man called, and the Lord heard him; he saved him out of all his troubles. The angel of the Lord encamps around those who fear him, and

he delivers them. Taste and see that the Lord is good;
blessed is the one who takes refuge in him. (84)

In Jesus Name, Amen.

Complete

*For in him the whole fullness of deity dwells
bodily, and you have been filled in him, who
is the head of all rule and authority.*

Colossians 2:9-10

Awareness

Without God we are lost, wandering in a world

without guidance. We may have our parents, role models,

and mentors but they pale in comparison to having the

guidance, protection, and provision of the almighty King

of Kings. So to simply be aware of his presence affords

us confidence, peace of mind, the ability to be kind and

forgiving, and the strength to move forward no matter

what life brings our way.

*For a day in your courts is better than a thousand
elsewhere. I would rather be a doorkeeper in
the house of my God than dwell in the tents of
wickedness. For the Lord God is a sun and shield;
the Lord bestows favor and honor. No good thing
does he withhold from those who walk uprightly. O
Lord of hosts, blessed is the one who trusts in you!*

Psalm 84:10 - 12

All is Well with My Soul

When it is all said and done and we have lived our

lives to its last moment, we can rest in knowing that to be

absent from the body is to be present with the Lord. God

is our light and our salvation, he is our burden bearer,

he sent his son Jesus to save us and Jesus has done just

that. There is no greater peace than to know that God is

for us, that we are forgiven, that we are the apple of his

eye, and that he loves us - immensely. More importantly,

how we rest eternally is of great importance, and knowing

that God considers us, not even worthy, but loved and

accepted is a gift that we cannot even fully realize until it

comes to pass.

While I am certain we are not all that God desires for us to be, he is developing our character each and every day. He is transforming our hearts and our minds so that when our life is over, and we meet him in heaven, he can welcome us with open arms, and say, "Well done, good and faithful servant."

And I am sure of this, that he who began a good work in you will bring it to completion at the day of Jesus Christ.

Philippians 1:6

Walking in Purpose

There is always a spiritual battle taking place and we have elected to walk with God, courtesy of the gift of salvation afforded by Jesus Christ. As those who have elected Christ as their Lord and Savior, we have the power of the Holy Spirit at work within us. The presence of God within us blesses us to be a blessing to others. God plants seeds of desire in our hearts that align with His will. We may not realize that God has planted the seed, but he will open doors that allow us to walk in our purpose, and for his greater good.

When Sampson begged his parents to marry a Philistine woman, he had no idea that it was in the will of God for him to do so - it was simply a desire placed in his heart. In the same way, when we belong to God, we become arrows in the hand of God, an instrument to help Him strategically accomplish what must be done.

God is with us. He not only directs our path, he goes before us to ensure that every crooked place is straight. He has prepared those we will encounter to bless us abundantly. God is our shield and our exceedingly great reward.

Now may the God of peace who brought again from the dead our Lord Jesus, the great shepherd of the sheep, by the blood of the eternal covenant, equip you with everything good that you may do his will, working in us that which is pleasing in his sight, through Jesus Christ, to whom be glory forever and ever. Amen.

Hebrews 13:20-21

God's promise is to be with us at all times; our

ability to discern his presence brings confidence, accept his love and walk in divine purpose are the gifts we receive in his presence.

Prayer

Most Gracious and Heavenly Father,

Thank you. Your presence shifts the atmosphere and our recognition of your presence provides security. Your love is greater than any love we may receive from man.

"You are my witnesses," declares the Lord, "and my servant whom I have chosen, so that you may know and believe me and understand that I am he. Before me no god was formed, nor will there be one after me. I, even I, am the Lord, and apart from me there is no savior. I have revealed and saved and proclaimed—I, and not some foreign god among you. You are my witnesses," declares the Lord, "that I am God. Yes, and from ancient days I am he. No one can deliver out of my hand. When I act, who can reverse it?"(85)

In Jesus Name, Amen.

בטחה *the* P R O M I S E

Citations

1. https://www.better-health.vic.gov.au/health/conditionsandtreatments/heart
2. I John 4:16
3. Jeremiah 29:13
4. James 4:8
5. Psalm 140:13
6. Genesis 28:15
7. Psalm 27:4
8. Psalm 28:7-8
9. 2 Corinthians 12:9-10
10. Mark 12:30
11. Nahum 1:2
12. Psalm 37:1-3
13. Deuteronomy 6:15
14. Song of Solomon 8: 6-7
15. Philippians 1:6
16. Galatians 5:10
17. 2 Peter 1:10
18. Jeremiah 17:7
19. 2 Thessalonians 3:16
20. Isaiah 26:3
21. Isaiah 12:2
22. Colossians 3:15
23. Psalm 5:12
24. Isaiah 41:10
25. Psalm 119:114
26. Psalm 5:11
27. Psalm 20:1
28. Exodus 33:13-14
29. Exodus 33: 16-19
30. Psalm 145
31. I Chronicles 29:11
32. Timothy 6:12-16
33. Luke 10:9
34. I Corinthians 4:20
35. 2 Corinthians 12:9
36. Colossians 1:11
37. I Corinthians 2:5
38. https://biblehub.com/q/what_is_the_shekinah_glory.htm#:~:text=Sum-mary%20of%20the%20Shekinah's%20mpor-tance,devotion%2C%20prompting%20awe%20and%20gratitude.
39. John 1:14
40. John 1:16-17
41. Hebrews 1:3
42. Matthew 6:33
43. Psalm 25:9
44. Romans 8:28
45. Isaiah 30:15a
46. Matthew 11:29
47. I Timothy 1:7
48. Ephesians 2:8-9
49. Isaiah 50:7
50. Isaiah 40:31
51. Numbers 14:18
52. I Kings 3:9
53. I John 2:10
54. I John 4:16
55. Ecclesiastes 11:7
56. 2 Samuel 23:4
57. Psalm 86
58. https://www.gold-ennumber.net/nautilus-spiral-golden-ratio/
59. Proverbs 3:5-6
60. Ephesians 2:4-10
61. https://allpoetry.com/The-Rose-That-Grew-From-Concrete

62. Colossians 3:17
63. Isaiah 43:1-21
64. Psalm 46
65. https://engediresource-center.com/2015/07/02/metzudah-god-is-our-refuge/#gsc.tab=0
66. 2 Samuel 22
67. Isaiah 11:2
68. John 14:15-17
69. 2 Corinthians 3:17
70. Romans 15:13
71. Romans 5:5
72. Psalm 131
73. I Chronicles 16:8-27

74. Psalm 75
75. Psalm 23
76. Philippians 4:4-9
77. Isaiah 40:28-31
78. https://www.hymnal.net/en/hymn/h/313
79. I John 1:5-10
80. Psalm 116:5-9
81. 2 John 1:1-6
82. Mark 10:46
83. Psalm 115
84. Psalm 34: 1-7
85. Isaiah 43:10-1

At the age of 9, Stephanie was molested by a friend of my family. In high school, she held the hand of a friend as he died from a fatal gun shot wound... As an adult, she was the victim of a violent acquaintance rape. Subsequently, she struggled with personal demons. But when she sought the Lord and his Word, her life was forever changed.

I give God ALL the Glory!

He is and will always be the head of my life. He is my joy, my strength, my everything. My constant prayer is to be a perfect conduit of his message and love.

stephanie moore

Stephanie was born in Muskogee, Oklahoma. She graduated from Putnam City North High School in 1994. She is the mother of 3 beautiful daughters, and has a grandson named Levi and a granddaughter named LaTrice. She holds an Associate of Arts in Applied Technology, a Bachelor of Arts in Communications, and a Master of Arts in Communication with an emphasis in Political Communication. Ms. Moore holds several design and technology certifications and has won numerous awards in that area. Stephanie has worked in television, print and web media for more than 20 years.

She is the owner of Moore Marketing and Communications. Her company offers strategic marketing and communication plans, media purchases, public relations, writing services, print services, graphic design and web design. Stephanie has also served as a poltical consultant for Governor, Lt. Governor, State Representative, Mayoral and City Council candidates.

Stephanie is also the founder of She's a BOSSE (A Beautiful Oasis of Success, Style and Elegance).

MY GOD
Psalm 63:1–?

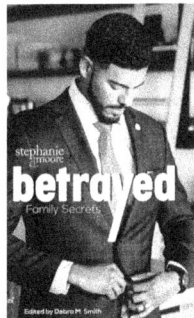

stephanie d. moore

NON-NEGOTIABLE BLESSINGS
SUPERNATURAL BLESSINGS FROM GOD

stephanie d. moore

OBEY
by stephanie d. moore

31 Day Devotional

stephanie d. moore
believe. confess. act.
RIGHT NOW! FAITH

TARES AMONG WHEAT
stephanie moore

A 31-Day Devotional
stephanie d. moore
THE BLESSING & THE CURSE
ISOLATION

The Living Proof!
A 31-DAY DEVOTIONAL
stephanie d.

stephanie d. moore
Without a DOUBT
ENTERING GOD'S REST

stephanie d. moore
Where is YOUR God?

ZION
stephanie d. moore
The Fortified & Holy City of God
A 31-Day Devotional

god is faithful!
blush
A 31-DAY DEVOTIONAL
OF GOD'S UNENDING LOVE FOR YOU
stephanie d. moore

Make HIS Praise Glorious!
PRAYSE
SPEAK LIFE
stephanie d. moore
A 31-DAY DEVOTIONAL The Power of Prayer & Praise

SPEECHLESS
stephanie d. moore
"Father, if you are willing, take this cup from me;
yet not my will, but yours be done."

HIS favor
stephanie d.
It's not about obtaining HIS favor...
It's about recognizing you already have it!

ECHOES
stephanie d. moore

stephanie d. moore
betrayed
Family Secrets
Edited by Debra M. Smith

stephanie d. moore

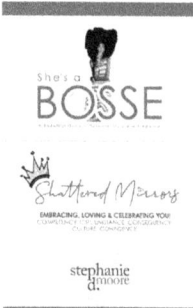

stephanie
d. moore